Imagine!
Ethical Digital Technology
For Everyone

First edition published 2023
by CRC Press
6000 Broken Sound Parkway NW, Suite 300, Boca Raton, FL 33487-2742
and by CRC Press
2 Park Square, Milton Park, Abingdon, Oxon, OX14 4RN

© Simon Rogerson
CRC Press is an imprint of Taylor & Francis Group, LLC

Library of Congress Cataloging-in-Publication Data
A catalog record has been requested for this title.

ISBN: (hbk) 978-1-032-42217-6
ISBN: (pbk) 978-1-032-42218-3
ISBN: (ebk) 978-1-003-36176-3
DOI: 10.1201/9781003361763

Designed by Simon Rogerson
Typeset by DerryField Publishing Services

To Anne

Love shields us

Love feeds us

Love entertains us

Love is at the very heart of us

Acknowledgements

Many of the creative pages contain components drawn from the vast library of images in Pixabay. The Pixabay license states: 'Content on Pixabay is made available to you on the following terms ('Pixabay License'). Under the Pixabay License you are granted an irrevocable, worldwide, non-exclusive and royalty-free right to use, download, copy, modify or adapt the Content for commercial or non-commercial purposes. Attribution of the photographer, videographer, musician or Pixabay is not required but is always appreciated'. In particular, figurines used as 'guides' in the book were downloaded from Pixabay. My thanks to Peggy and Marco Lachmann-Anke who have created a fantastic collection of these characters. They can be accessed at https://pixabay.com/users/peggy_marco-1553824/

I wish to record my thanks to John Wyzalek, who is the Senior Acquisitions Editor at Taylor & Francis/CRC Press. From the moment I contacted John with my idea for the first book in the trilogy, he has offered tremendous support, help and encouragement. His enthusiastic acceptance of my vision to create this unusual trilogy has enabled me to turn this into a reality.

My thanks to Theron R. Shreve, Director, DerryField Publishing Services, for his advice in creating and formatting this third book and to Susan Culligan for her help in finalising the book for production.

Finally, I wish to thank Katharine Short, Special Collections Manager, Directorate of Library and Learning Services, De Montfort University, UK. Without any hesitation, Katharine accepted my collection of papers, books and other artefacts for the University Archive. She showed me how to create an archive index so that I could deliver the collection in a structured form. It was through this activity that I realised my works had the potential to be published as a trilogy. Without Katharine's involvement, I doubt the trilogy would have surfaced!

Contents

Foreword

The book that you have in your hands, or on your device, will take you on an amazing journey. You are going to travel through an unexplored landscape: the ethical and social jungle of digital technology. You will travel avoiding typical mass-tourism and gentrification and skip dominant technological determinism. Instead of having 'a typical journey', you will discover unexplored corners of digital technology from a humanistic point of view. Welcome aboard!

Perhaps you continue this journey because you started with the other books of the *Ethical Digital Technology Trilogy*. When you see that a book is part of a trilogy, you might question yourself whether you should have read the previous books to be able to follow this one. If *Imagine! Ethical Digital Technology For Everyone* is your first reading of the trilogy, you will not find any barriers against accessing and enjoying the book. If you have previously read *The Evolving Landscape of Ethical Digital Technology* and/or *Ethical Digital Technology in Practice*, welcome back. In this book you will find a completely different approach that will allow you to enrich the previous analyses. Professor Rogerson wrote the trilogy completing a perfect circle, and so it does not matter if you read this book as the first one, the last one, or standalone. If this is your second or last reading of the trilogy, you will find an original perspective of digital ethics from an aesthetic based on the arts and imagination. If this is your first reading of the trilogy, you will enter the topic of digital ethics from a very imaginative and open approach that will probably motivate you to read the other books of the trilogy later. If you are reading only this book, you will find many insights leading you to consider and question our current digital lives.

As in any other journey, you are going to enjoy thoughts and feelings that will open a new perspective on, in this case, digital technology. You will enjoy pictures, poems, stories, and quotations that should encourage self-reflection and community discussion about your real life, your digital life, and the role of technology in society. It is assumed widely by society that the digital technology revolution has a positive impact on our welfare. But what do you know about the dark side of technology? Probably not much, because, as Professor Rogerson writes in this book, in 1995 he realised that 'technology has evolved from a coercive technology to a seductive technology'. Seductive technologies have conquered us. We are living in love with them without questioning any potential negative impact, which indeed they do have. What about key issues in digital ethics, such as technological dependency, privacy, free choice, rights and justice and the digital divide? Are you aware of your digital shadow? As Professor Rogerson wrote in 2003, digital shadows, which don't disappear when the light is over, can have unimaginable uses by organisations with potentially undesirable consequences. Drawbacks of technology are often hidden. This book steers us towards a critical thinking of technology, making visible the invisible dark side of digitalisation. For instance, this might include reducing the interaction between people, fostering isolation, or discovering the emerging challenges that should be overcome concerning the distribution of responsibilities between humans (vendors, users and developers) and ICT (hardware and software) when technology has the potential to harm humans.

In the current digital environment, ethics, law and government are reactive, as they are lagging behind the deployment and commercialisation of digital technology. That gap means that technology usually is not aligned with ethics and societal values, requiring a proactive approach in which people and education must play a key role. People must be in the core of the digital revolution. A poem written by Professor Rogerson, included in this book, explains clearly why: 'People make things, People change things, People use things, People abuse things'; and because of that, it is necessary that technical disciplines enrich their approaches from an interdisciplinary perspective to reach an ethical development of digital technologies and their applications.

Professor Rogerson's thoughts and ideas are combined and contrasted with historical and contemporary poets, architects, writers and painters such as Simonides (c.556–468 BC), Van Gogh (1853–1890), and Jorge Luis Borges (1899–1986). While reading the book, we can see that despite the digital revolution and its huge transformative impacts on individuals and society, human nature itself has changed little, and we must strive to guarantee that digital technology is not going to pervert our human nature. Ethics should be the driver of the digital transformation if we desire to preserve our essence as humans and continue developing a better society for us all. As Professor Rogerson wrote in 2022, *'Digital technology can add value to life, but it can also take value away from life'*. To add value to life, Professor Rogerson stresses the need to develop a rich picture of digital systems development, in which people and education should be the in the centre to guarantee that the impact of any digital system and applications is right for society.

Concluding, you will find in this book a fascinating critical analysis about digital technology from a humanistic perspective. As the title implies, it is an imaginative approach about ethical digital technology that is interesting for everyone. Professor Rogerson's concerns about digital technology began when the digital technology jungle was at the very beginning of its exponential growth. The first time that I met Simon Rogerson was at the end of the 1990s in the Centre for Computing and Social Responsibility (De Montfort University). He opened my mind to the hidden side of digital technology. Simon has created a school of thought in the information ethics field. Considering, as the Van Gogh quote included in the preface of this book, states *'The beginning is perhaps more difficult than anything else'*, I believe that his efforts in the digital forum are worthy of praise. This book is oriented towards anyone and everyone, breaking academic and professional barriers, thereby increasing universal awareness of the importance of the ethical concerns surrounding digital technology.

In your journey of exploration into digital ethics, you can read each section consecutively, or as Simon suggests to readers, *'Open the book at random—each item has a story to tell'*. Either way, you will enjoy it. Are you ready to open your mind to challenge all forms of technological determinism? So, what are you waiting for? Enjoy your journey!

Mario Arias Oliva
21 December 2022

Mario Arias Oliva is Profesor Titular de Universidad Complutense de Madrid. He holds two PhDs related to business, marketing and the impact of digital technology. He is currently Vice Principal of the Marketing Department in the Faculty of Economics and Business. He is a leading figure in the digital ethics community associated with the ETHICOMP conference series, holding steering committee membership and having been a conference director three times.

Preface

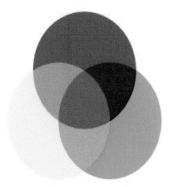

My Artistic Lineage

Margaret Hamilton
Great Grandmother
(b 1843) aged 21

John Hamilton Rogerson
Grandfather
(b 1875) aged 14

1864

1864

George Rogerson
Father
(b 1916) aged 13; 15; 25

Simon Rogerson
(b 1951) aged 14; 69; 71

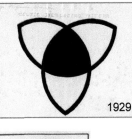

1929

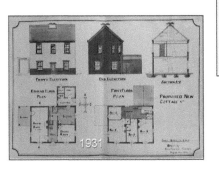

1931

1941

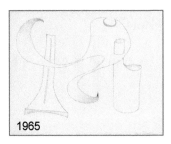

1965

2020

Eileen Joyce Rogerson
Mother
(b 1918) aged 60

1978

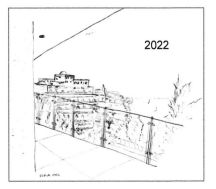

2022

Reflection and imagination through the eyes of Vincent Van Gogh (1853-1890)

- What would life be if we had no courage to attempt anything?

- The beginning is perhaps more difficult than anything else.

- We spend our whole lives in unconscious exercise of the art of expressing our thoughts with the help of words.

- We are surrounded by poetry on all sides.

- I am always doing what I cannot do yet, in order to learn how to do it.

- Normality is a paved path: it's comfortable to walk but no flowers grow there.

- It is looking at things for a long time that ripens you and gives you a deeper meaning.

- I have nature and art and poetry, and if that is not enough, what is enough?

- Do not quench your inspiration and your imagination.

STEM Evolution

Science

Technology

Engineering

Art

Maths

-

Ethics

Responsibility   STEAM-ER

 [2020]

Chimerical Algorithms

Ada grew up with computer technology. In fact she was even named after one of its pioneers, Ada Lovelace. Howard, her father, had worked on some of the early computers. He met her mother, Grace, whilst serving in the armed forces, working on the ADA programming language, which was used in military defence applications. Grace was involved in computer programming too and had worked on developing COBOL, the COmmercial Business-Oriented Language.

So it was hardly surprising that Ada had always loved programming, for it was in her blood. It was a world of logic, certainty and objectivity. Pouring over lines of code never failed to excite and motivate. She delighted in producing programs which included precisely defined rules to solve problems of all kinds. Back home, Ada relaxed, letting her unchecked imagination create a fantasy world which she shared with her fellow geeks through her *Chimerical Algorithms Blog* on the *Seek Geek* social network.

Ada's latest blog entry, *Kate's eight plus two – 1010-12-A,* contained a group of carefully crafted items:

- **Parrot**—Nicknamed Pretty Polly, a method for painting the town red, and blue, and yellow, and green, and any other colour you care to mention.

- **Cherry**—Method for cleaning dirty shoes with boot polish so they blossom.

- **Rhubarb**—A political procrastination tactic similar to filibustering—rhubarb, rhubarb, rhubarb!

- **Jealousy**—A computer games algorithm used by programmers to incorporate green-eyed monsters into the characters.

- **Thighs**—The procedural acronym for sustaining a better society:

  o   be Truthful

  o   be Honest

  o   exhibit Integrity

  o   be Good

  o   act with Humility

  o   be Sensitive

  known as *Thighs of Relief*

Chimerical Algorithms continued

- **Carousel**—An iterative process for sorting items in a roundabout way.

- **Addiction**—A method of enunciation in speech to promote the adoption of common language such as Esperanto.

- **Champagne**—An artificial intelligence algorithm for identifying personality traits, nicknamed Bubbly.

- **Carrot**—A process for providing psychological assistance for medics—euphemistically known as *What's up doc?*

- **Pirate**—Taxation method for specialist food manufacture of soft-top pies—called by the Press *The Pukka Tax*.

Ada finished her blog with a little algorithmic poem she thought would amuse her geek friends:

Start

Go home

Eat

Take feet off ground

Let mind wander

Capture imagination

Come back down to earth

Sleep

Waken

Go to work

End

Life itself is a quotation.
Jorge Luis Borges 1899–1986

Painting is silent poetry,
poetry is eloquent painting.
Simonides c.556–468 BC

Quotation

Poem

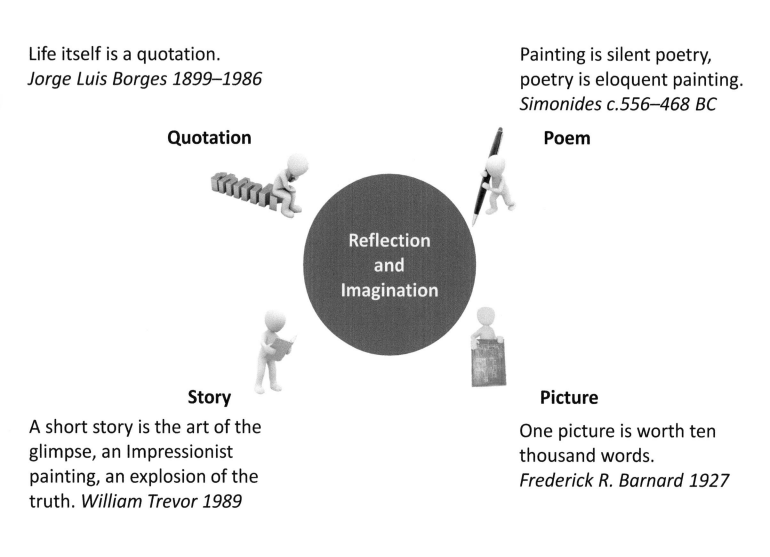

Reflection
and
Imagination

Story

A short story is the art of the
glimpse, an Impressionist
painting, an explosion of the
truth. *William Trevor 1989*

Picture

One picture is worth ten
thousand words.
Frederick R. Barnard 1927

1 Introduction

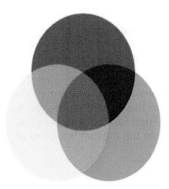

The *Ethical Digital Technology Trilogy* is the product of my research stretching back to 1995. As such it is a ground-breaking synthesis drawing on a plethora of historical evidence while firmly focused on the future. It explores the landscape of digital technology from a social-impact perspective. The contrasting approaches in the three books allow access to this landscape by everyone: academics, practitioners and the public at large, regardless of age. The key message is that digital ethics should underpin and indeed drive the development and use of digital technology. The trilogy's three interrelated perspectives provide a unique holistic view of how society is becoming increasingly dependent on digital technology and how this dependency must be managed to ensure societally positive rather than societally negative outcomes.

The third book, *Imagine! Ethical Digital Technology for Everyone,* is about science and technology meeting the creative arts to open access and engage with everyone as the world becomes more and more technologically dependent. It aligns with the transition of STEM (Science, Technology, Engineering and Mathematics) to STEAM (Science, Technology, Engineering, Arts and Mathematics), which aims to promote creativity and curiosity. The book contains pictures, poems, stories and quotations about the social and ethical issues surrounding digital technology. I have created all this material, and as such it is a unique offering in the field. There has never been anything like this before.

This creative book is accessible to everyone of all ages. There is something here for everyone. Each page covers a standalone issue or focus. It invites the reader to reflect and look beyond the obvious. Overall, there are running themes and messages about how to realise ethical digital technology. These become more transparent as the reader travels through the book.

There are four creative forms used:

Pictures: These tend to be diagrams or schematics which highlight relationships. Some of these schematics use rich picture techniques from the Soft Systems Methodology.

Poems: Ethical issues surrounding digital technology are explored through the use of a variety of poetical forms.

Stories: Each story is a fictitious account of an ethically charged situation which could arise since the digital technology exists to enable the reported event.

Quotations: These quotations, taken from my papers and presentations, are grouped together to act as a catalyst for ethical reflection.

There are approximately 100 creative pages based on my work dating from 1975 through to the present day. For each item, the year in brackets [yyyy] was the year it was first conceived. Some modification or enhancement may have taken place since then, but the original concept remains intact.

Section 2 provides an account of the evolution of digital technology. Section 3 explores the ethical and societal challenges arising from this evolution. Section 4 offers some suggestions on how to approach realising ethical digital technology. Finally, Section 5, Food for Thought, provides some pointers and interpretations of all elements within each of the four creative forms. The letters in the bottom left hand corner of each element refer to the associated note in one of the four tables to be found in Section 5.

[2021]

B

Landscape Complexity

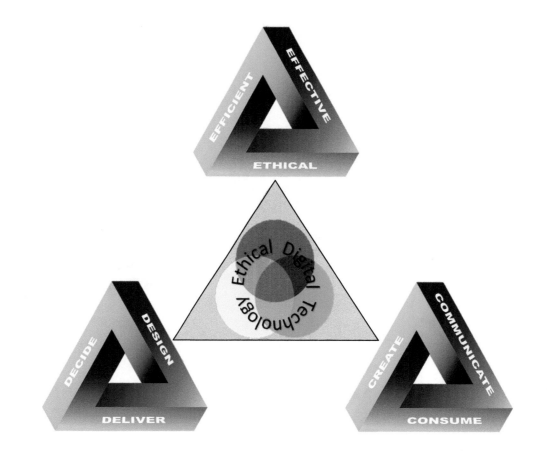

...

Three Perspectives

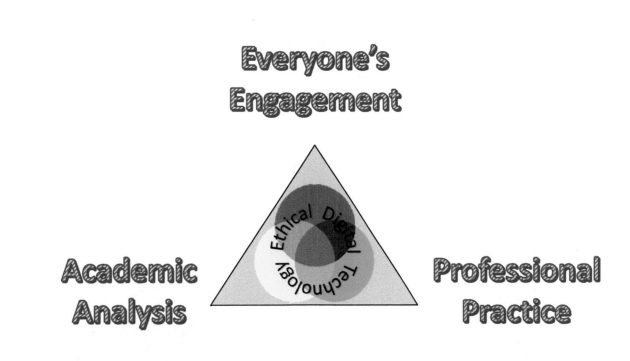

The Ethical Digital Technology Trilogy

Digital Ethics

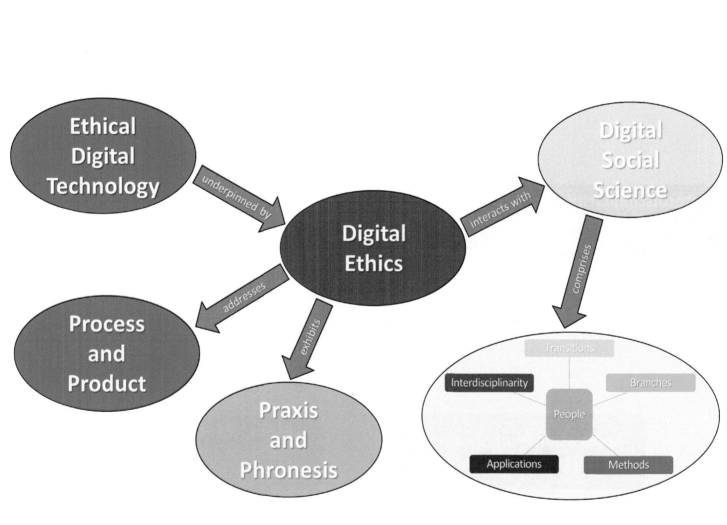

[2021]

The Pentagon of Digital Social Science

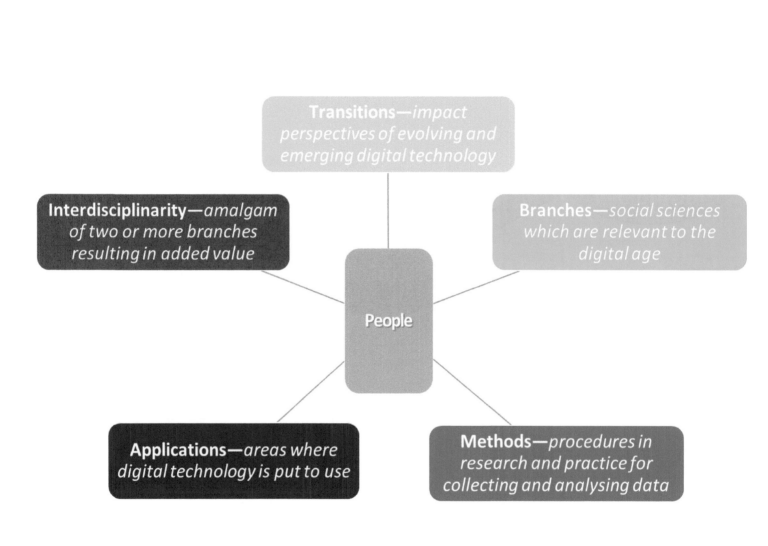

Transitions—*impact perspectives of evolving and emerging digital technology*

Interdisciplinarity—*amalgam of two or more branches resulting in added value*

Branches—*social sciences which are relevant to the digital age*

People

Applications—*areas where digital technology is put to use*

Methods—*procedures in research and practice for collecting and analysing data*

[2021]

thrice, triplet or triangle

lessons, landscape and language

Aristotle, Autonomy, Artificial

Bad, Bentham, Back Door

Create, Communicate, Consume

Duty, Digital Divide

Efficient, Effective, Ethical

Fraud, Flame, Free Speech

Good, Google, Global

Honesty, Hacker, Holistic

Information, Intelligence, Integrity

Justice, Judgement, Jargon

Knowledge, Kant, Key Escrow

Law, Logic, Locke

Moral, Millennial, Microsoft

Neural, Netiquette, Non-Malfeasance

Obligation, Overload, Open Source

Product, Process, Purpose

Quantum, Question, Quality

Right, Rigour, Responsibility

Society, Security, Spam

Trust, Trusting, Trustworthy

Ubiquitous, Utility, Unethical

Virtue, Virtual, Virus

World Wide Web

Xbox, Generation X, XEROX

Yahoo, Generation Y, Y2K

Zoom, Zen, Generation Z

DEBEE's A-2-Zee!

A

[2020]

Famous architect Frank Ching once wrote, 'The visual data received by the eye is processed, manipulated and filtered by the mind in its active search for structure and meaning'.

It's time to take a journey of reflection and imagination through the realms of digital technology.

Open the book at random—each item has a story to tell. Read the book from start to finish and you'll discover overall themes and messages.

Take your feet off the ground and let your mind wander.

What impact does digital technology have on you and others?

Is this going to change in the future?

Enjoy the exploration!

A

2 Digital Technology

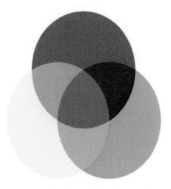

Important Moments in Computer Science History

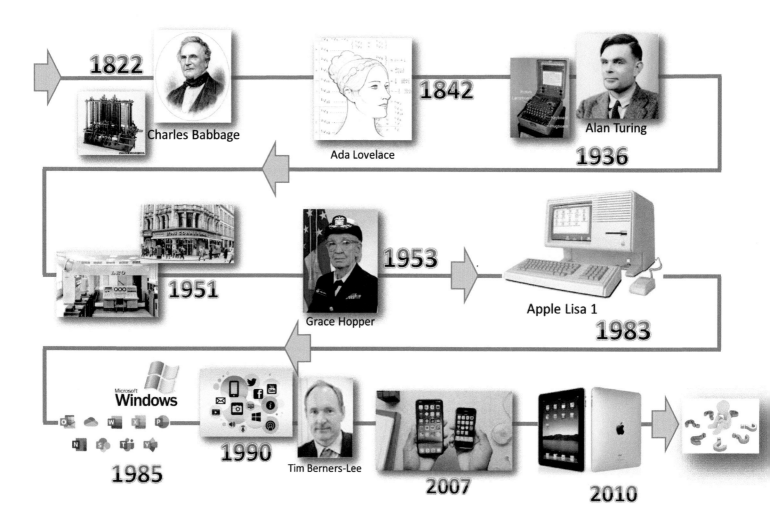

1822 — Charles Babbage

1842 — Ada Lovelace

1936 — Alan Turing

1951 — LEO

1953 — Grace Hopper

1983 — Apple Lisa 1

1985 — Microsoft Windows

1990 — Tim Berners-Lee

2007

2010

The Birth of the Information Age

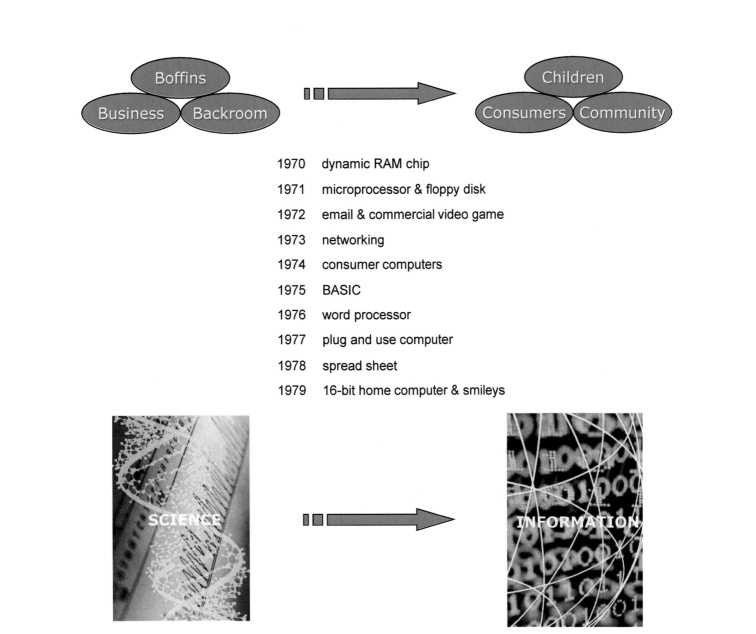

1970   dynamic RAM chip

1971   microprocessor & floppy disk

1972   email & commercial video game

1973   networking

1974   consumer computers

1975   BASIC

1976   word processor

1977   plug and use computer

1978   spread sheet

1979   16-bit home computer & smileys

[2008]

The Rhyming ICT Miscellany

addICT—computer nerd with obsessive will
convICT—cybercriminal with pockets to fill

contradICTion—system error likely a fatal fault
afflICTion—computer bug everything grinds to a halt

evICT—delete files not required
verdICT—output results so desired

restrICTion—cybersecurity all under lock and key
benedICTion—data protection means privacy for you and me

derelICT—system obsolescence the queue to scrap
vICTory—successful implementation the progress map

fICTion—virtual reality is all around
dICTate—speech recognition translates sound

[2021]

Converting Technologies

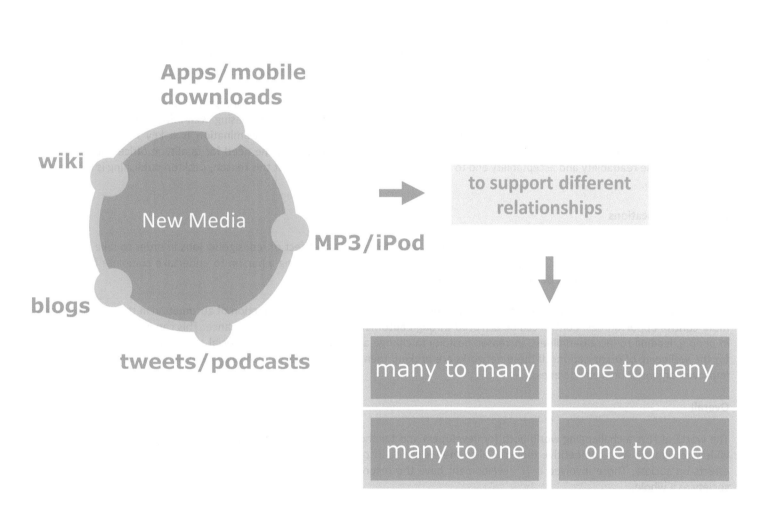

[2008]

The World of Information Technology

IT and the competitive edge

It is widely recognised that IT can be used to achieve a competitive edge. The key to successful application is in ensuring that IT serves business objectives and opportunities. The range of applications is extremely diverse and is continually broadening.

In the manufacturing sector, companies have spent millions of pounds introducing computer integrated manufacturing (CIM) into their production processes. In the retail sector, intense competition and the demands of increasing well-informed and service-oriented consumers have forced organisations to invest heavily in IT. Effective information dissemination is a key factor to survival and advancement in today's information society. There has been increasing awareness of the need for quality in office documentation in order to increase readability and acceptability and to aid the dissemination process. For this reason, desktop publishing is fast becoming a growth IT area.

The social implications

IT may reduce the interaction between people, perhaps as an unforeseen side effect of redesigning jobs in order to take full economic advantage of the new technology. For example, a job which is enhanced, so allowing a person to undertake complete functions, may reduce the opportunities for that person to talk and meet with others.

A feeling of isolation is bound to result, and the social network will be altered. The introduction of automation in the workplace creates more control opportunities. Control can be achieved through automatic monitoring of performance. This can invoke anxiety and stress in people, leading to increased illness, increased hostility to change and a breakdown in the social structure. Social networks are vital for the wellbeing of organisations. If these networks are broken, then hostility towards technology will be promoted at the expense of improved organisational effectiveness.

Overall

The world of IT is a challenging world both for developers and for those who use IT products and services. Information Technology is widely recognised as a competitive tool crucial to the wellbeing of organisations. It is a technology which can have detrimental side effects on society. Those involved in IT development have the responsibility of ensuring that IT is used wisely for organisations and society as a whole.

[1988]

Is it raining?

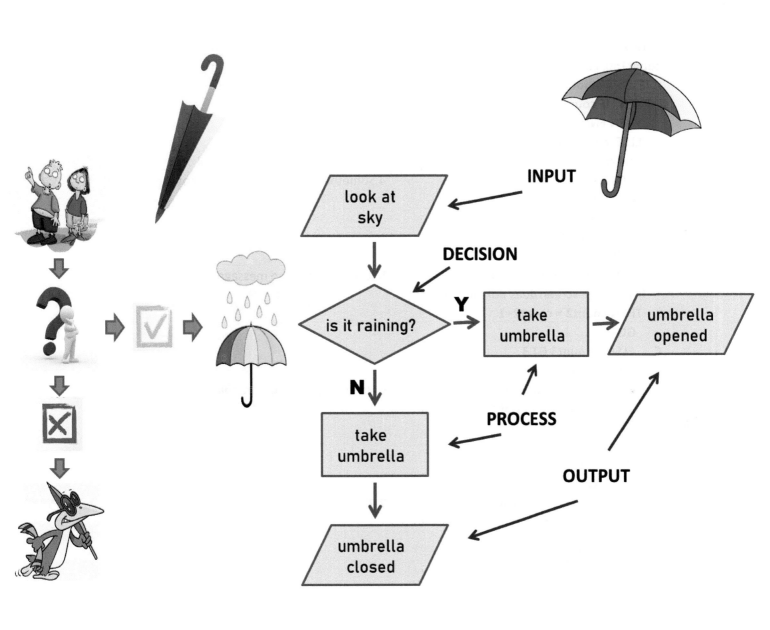

H

[2020]

Poetical Programming

Pseudocode & Boolean Logic [precise]	Comment Lines & Use Case [fuzzy]
BEGIN	"1 Of message texting he was a fan"
count1=0, count2=0, count3=0	"2 Hidden logic exists so he can"
A IF mobile not on	
THEN IF count1 GT 3	
THEN END	
ELSE count1=count1+1	
switch on	"3 Switches on mobile then signal check"
GOTO A	"4 Something's not working, oh what the heck"
ELSE IF no signal	
THEN END	
B ELSE IF count2 GT 3	
THEN END	
ELSE press messaging icon	"5 It springs to life so message chosen"
IF message screen does not appear	
THEN count2 = count2+1	
GOTO B	
C ELSE IF count3 GT 3	
THEN END	
ELSE press new message icon	"6 He quickly starts before things frozen"
IF new message does not appear	
THEN count3=count3+1	
GOTO C	
ELSE choose 'enter recipient'	
choose 'contact list'	
IF recipient in contact list	"7 Billy's number not in contact list"
THEN select recipient number	
GOTO D	
ELSE IF not know recipient number	
THEN END	

[2014]

Poetical Programming continued

Pseudocode & Boolean Logic [precise]	Comment Lines & Use Case [fuzzy]
ELSE key in number	"8 He keys it in so texting not missed"
D choose 'enter message'	"9 Lets Billy know of situation"
E IF message incomplete	"10 Through this text of his own creation"
THEN key in message	"11 Hi there Billy it's a little chilly
GOTO E	/12 Heating broken since we've spoken
ELSE IF attachment required	/13 Not yet mended 'cos on gas man depended
THEN press attachment icon	/14 Got on layers of clothes from head to toes"
select type	
select attachment	"15 Adds a selfie of him dressed to kill"
go back to message	
send message	
END	"16 Sends text before he catches a chill"
ELSE send message	
END	
END	

Note: Pseudocode uses the structural conventions of a programming language but is intended for human reading rather than machine reading. In computer programming, a comment is a programming language construct used to embed programmer-readable annotations in the source code of a computer program. Boolean logic is a form of algebra in which all values are reduced to either TRUE or FALSE. A Use Case is a list of steps, typically defining interactions between a person and a system, to achieve a goal.

[2014]

Digital Technology Systems

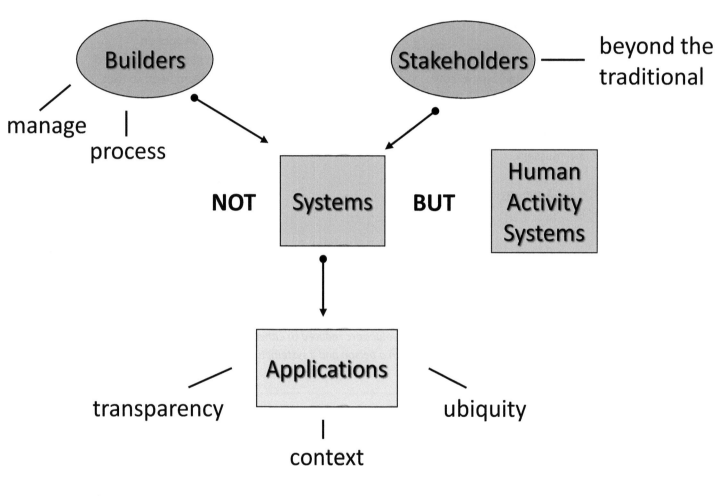

Builders

Stakeholders —— beyond the traditional

manage

process

NOT Systems BUT Human Activity Systems

Applications

transparency ubiquity

context

[2001]

Floodlighting Design System

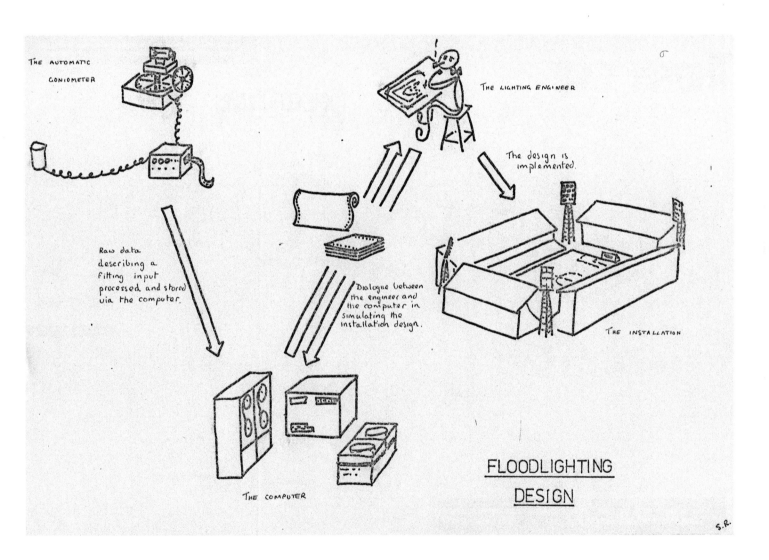

THE AUTOMATIC GONIOMETER

Raw data describing a fitting input processed and stored via the computer.

THE COMPUTER

Dialogue between the engineer and the computer in simulating the installation design.

THE LIGHTING ENGINEER

The design is implemented.

THE INSTALLATION

FLOODLIGHTING DESIGN

S.R.

[1975]

Computerised Vehicle Scheduling

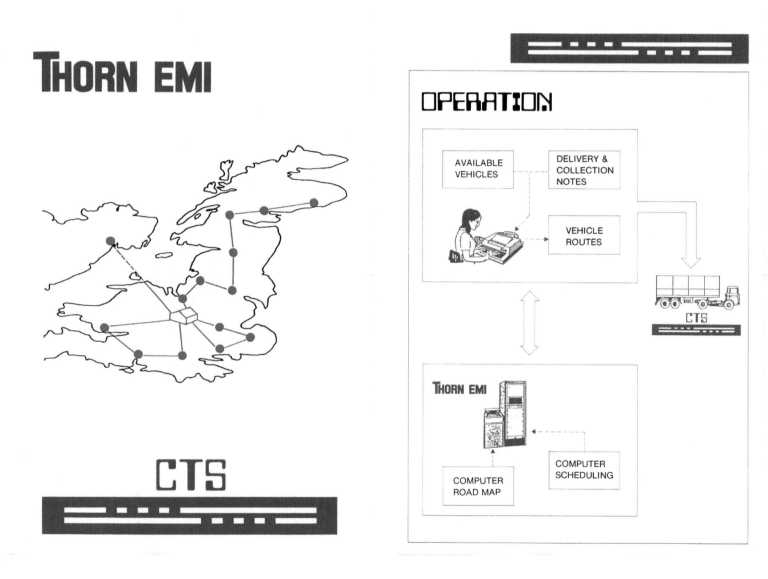

[1978]

Chemco

Chemco is a major producer of chemical compounds used by most UK manufacturing industries. It has several plants around the UK, usually located in sparsely populated regions. The exception to this is the newest plant, which is located in a major city in central England. This was opened 18 months ago and seen as the flagship plant using the latest chemical engineering techniques and heavily dependent on computer systems throughout production management. During the normal consultation process, the local community had expressed concerns about having such a plant within a densely populated region but had been reassured by the planned use of advanced technology to control the plant's operations.

Management of the new plant were encouraged to seek innovative ways in which to reduce the overhead costs of the plant. The use of the latest computer technology and software advances was seen as a key component of this innovative approach. The systems development team would focus on using expert system software based on either neural nets or fuzzy logic to automate the production runs and so increase throughput whilst reducing existing accepted numbers of production workers. There would be a significant increase in computer-controlled production. It was felt that the front-end input systems for triggering production were tried and tested in existing plants and that all that was needed to realise operational cost savings was to substitute the production control and monitoring subsystems, which required significant production worker intervention, with the new 'intelligent' subsystems.

There would be virtually no operator involvement once the production process was started until the reaction was complete and the chemical compounds were being channelled into the distribution holding tanks. Operators would also have an important role to play in keeping the plant clean, ensuring residues and waste were correctly disposed of. This cleaning-up process was not automated other than the computer-controlled valves which directed residue and waste away from the open drains. At other plants production workers had suggested that this clean-up phase could be linked automatically to the production phase, ensuring a smoother production cycle. Management had rejected this idea on the basis of cost.

The computer specialists and production managers agreed on a strategy and worked together to develop the new system. The system was tested using new sophisticated simulation software. It passed all tests which included normal running situations as well as abnormal running situations. The company looked forward to the new plant operating at a new level of efficiency. Following typical minor problems during the commissioning stage, the system had performed well during the first 18 months. Operating costs were well below the average for Chemco, and throughput had been increased by 12%.

[2000]

Chemco continued

It was the night shift at Chemco's newest plant. As usual the experienced laboratory worker activated the computer-based batch process input procedure to start the next chemical production. He inadvertently keyed in 'tank 593' rather than 'tank 693', which introduced the wrong chemical into the production run. The computer system was not designed to capture automatically such errors, other than having a data input correction facility if such an error occurred. This was the way the input subsystem worked in other Chemco plants. Experienced laboratory workers were able to double check the data and make adjustments as necessary.

On this occasion in the new plant the result was disastrous. The incorrect chemical resulted in a temperature rise in the reactor vat, leading to a rupture and subsequent explosion. An administrator observing the error was unable to contact the production operator in time to prevent the accident. The operator did not have the facility to ease the rise in temperature, and the new subsystem did not cover this aspect of the production process. The operator summoned the plant's fire brigade. Members of the fire brigade underestimated the danger involved and were not wearing the prescribed safety equipment. They bore the brunt of the explosion. Three people died and nine were seriously injured. There was a wider problem as well. The chemicals spilling from the ruptured vat leaked into the local drainage system before the computer-controlled valves closed. Harmful chemicals contaminated water over a three mile radius from the plant.

Chemco's initial reaction to the disaster was to acknowledge the tragic outcome both for the employees and their families as well as those living in close proximity to the plant. They were keen to stress that the accident had been caused by a series of human errors by Chemco workers on the night shift. The computer specialists, whilst generally upset about the disaster, felt relieved that the system they had developed and implemented was not seen as a cause of the accident. In the days immediately after the accident, there were growing calls for a public inquiry.

[2000]

C

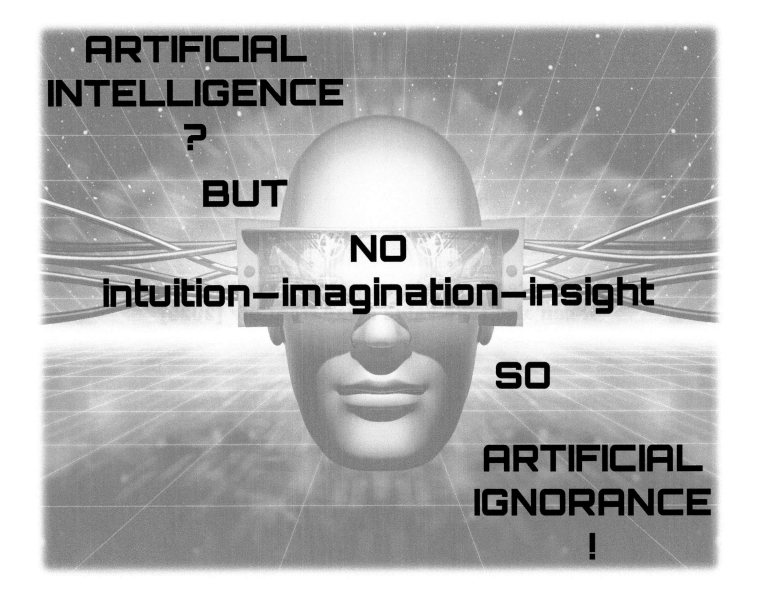

[2021]

L

Digital technology can add value to life, but it can also take value away from life [2022]

Points to Ponder

Digital Technology Projects

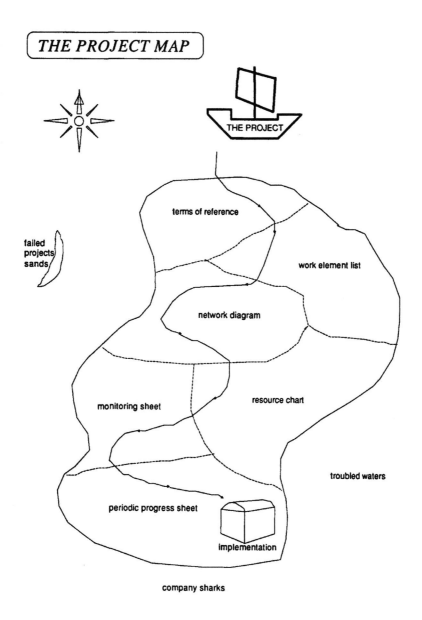

THE PROJECT MAP

THE PROJECT

terms of reference

failed projects sands

work element list

network diagram

monitoring sheet

resource chart

troubled waters

periodic progress sheet

implementation

company sharks

M

[1989]

ICT Relationship Trinity

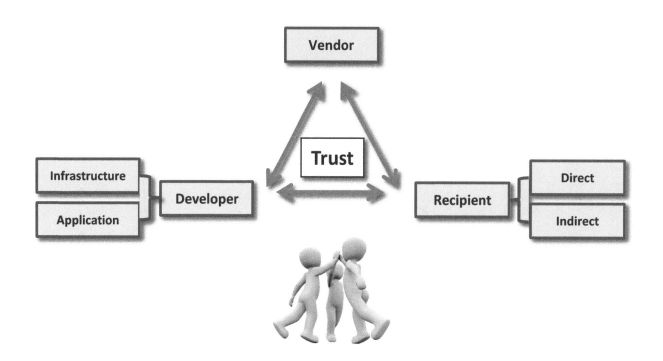

[2013]

There is no single solution
to a given problem [1985]

Usually projects fail not because of a
single major catastrophe but through a
combination of poor work practices
and poorly executed techniques [1989]

Evolution will be more acceptable and
sustainable than an apocalyptic
approach [1993]

C

Creating Professional Codes

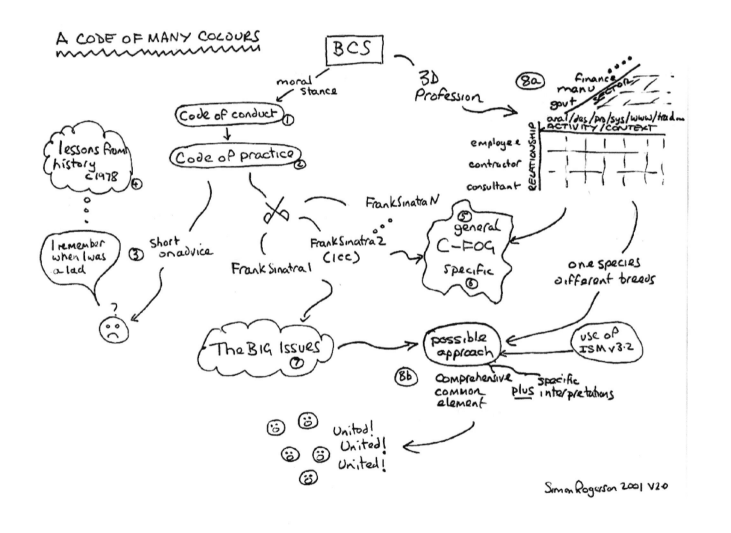

[2001]

Rich Picture of Systems Development

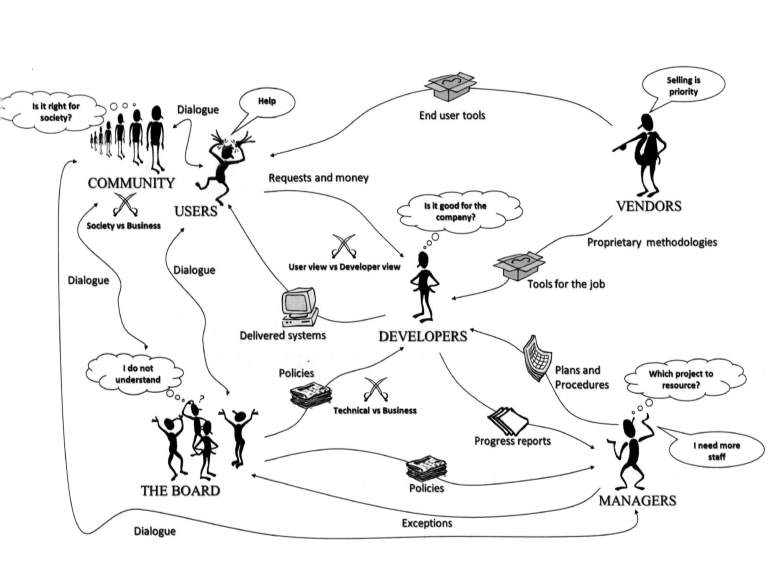

[1995]

Technology has evolved from a coercive technology to a seductive technology [1995]

Unreliable information and unstable information systems will lead to information bankruptcy [1998]

One solution is no solution [2011]

Points to Ponder

D

3 Issues and Contexts

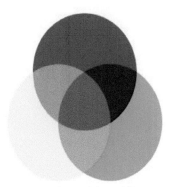

Technological Dependency

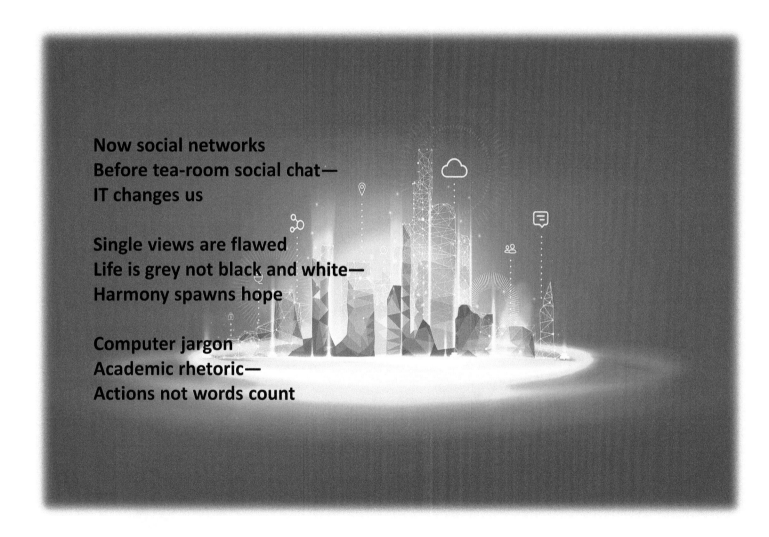

Now social networks
Before tea-room social chat—
IT changes us

Single views are flawed
Life is grey not black and white—
Harmony spawns hope

Computer jargon
Academic rhetoric—
Actions not words count

D

[2015]

Garage Auction Website

Auction sales on the Internet were growing rapidly and were forecast to represent nearly 25% of online retail sales within a couple of years. This promising prospect led Wendy Jones to establish a new auction website, which she called GARAGE, which was aimed at attracting young people 16 to 25 years old. Wendy believed that this age group had the greatest potential sales growth. She carefully analysed the functions and style of existing auction websites so that she could offer an alternative. She concluded that the site must have an anarchic, anti-establishment feel so that it would attract a lot of young people.

The business model for GARAGE was based on several key points:

- GARAGE would receive a fee from people who wanted to list and sell items for auction. It would charge a percentage of the final sales price for completed auctions.

- GARAGE would merely be a publisher, much like a newspaper that publishes classified advertisements, with no responsibility for transactions, since it would simply provide the conduit through which auction transactions could occur.

- GARAGE would not veto items posted for auction, but it would be marketed to ensure that posted items were of interest to the targeted age range. It was likely that some items would be controversial in the opinion of other age groups, and this was part of the marketing strategy.

- GARAGE users would be tracked, since this would be essential for growing the business. HTML e-mail would be sent to all those accessing the site. HTML email would act like a Web page, requesting graphics and content from a Web server and counting as a 'hit' on the GARAGE website. GARAGE would be able to track how and when people responded to email, note where they click, and trace follow-up actions on GARAGE pages.

- GARAGE would set up an advice service, called GI, on the products being auctioned. This would enable potential purchasers to find out more about the products offered. Those wishing to provide 'expert advice' would register with GI, giving contact details and a brief description of their credentials. Information providers would pay a fee for GI registration. In return a GI expert would receive a commission for each access of information they posted. The fee for completed sales would cover this commission.

Five weeks ago GARAGE was launched. It was an immediate success. The design of the site and the use of street language attracted many young people. By the end of four weeks, 7000 products had been sold. A typical virtual auction attracted around 1000 people worldwide. There were now 250 registered experts on GI. The products offered for auction included clothes, music, books, various equipment and appliances, adult items and recreational drugs. Controversy was growing about GARAGE, but it was this which seemed to be boosting the numbers of people using the site.

[2002]

Garage Auction Website continued

Last Friday, it was reported in the German national press that a 19-year-old man had killed a 25-year-old woman. The man was inquisitive about martial arts since playing his latest superheroes computer game featuring Bravado, a martial arts champion. He had come across a GARAGE auction of nunchaku sticks and throwing stars. Both were martial arts weapons. Using GI the man had found out how these weapons could be used and their relevance to martial-arts culture. According to the posted credentials, the GI expert who had posted the information had been a martial arts instructor for over ten years. The man purchased four throwing stars through the GARAGE auctioneer, who was based in the USA. Eager to try out his new acquisition, he went into his back yard to practise throwing the stars using the information he had obtained from GI. The stars need careful handling because they can be thrown long distances with relative ease. This was not indicated in the GI information. The man threw one of the stars very hard. It missed the target, veered to the right and hit the main artery in the neck of a woman who was walking down a public pathway some 50 metres away. The woman collapsed and tragically died in hospital through loss of blood.

On hearing the news, Wendy was sorry that the tragic accident had occurred, but she did not see how it could be blamed on GARAGE. She argued that these minor negative effects were symptomatic of the business model on which GARAGE was built. This feeling of being in a slightly risky, lawless environment in which you could purchase otherwise unavailable products was what was attracting such great numbers of young people to GARAGE. Indeed, she felt vindicated that her strategy was working.

[2002]

D

Machine: the Final Chapter

Computer
Bits, bytes, ones, zeros
So Charles and Ada conceive—
IT's Pandora's box

Robot
Man and beast replaced
Same task over and over—
Objective carnage

AI
Boolean bible
Artificial ignorance—
Logical ending

Evolutionary finale—Armageddon

E

[2019]

The Interactive Travel Portal

In the family home 350 km north west of Kuala Lumpur, Fai was asleep. Yi Siang and Layann sat down in front of their TV and switched into the Interactive Travel Portal (ITP). Having identified themselves, they were greeted by a smiling digital face of a woman.

'We want to get directions from our house to Kuala Lumpur'. Layann said. He gave the name of the hotel. It was their first holiday in three years. A combination of Fai, now an energetic toddler, and work had prevented them from taking time away up to now. Yi Siang was heavily pregnant with their second child, but both of them needed the holiday. They had decided to incorporate Hari Kebangsaan into their holiday.

'OK, Layann'. began the guide. 'A good way to do that is to . . .'

As the ITP guide spoke, detailed maps appeared on the screen to illustrate the spoken words. When finished, the guide asked if they wanted the directions stored and sent to their mobile phones. They eagerly agreed to this, starting to get excited about the trip, and the guide went on to say,

'If you would like, I can track your position through your mobile phone as you travel. This will allow me to guide you past traffic obstructions and send your position to your vehicle breakdown service should you have any problems. This will cost a one-off fee of RM 25. Are you interested?'

Yi Siang nodded and Layann said that they were. He instructed the service be directed to his phone. The guide asked them to wait while it checked for other information relevant to them and their trip. After a few seconds the guide announced,

'Yi Siang, I am informed by the Healthcare Patient Link (HPL) that there are health considerations you might want to take into account for this trip. Would you like to go to HPL now?'

Yi Siang agreed to this. The HPL site, represented by a little cartoon doctor, welcomed her. Commenting on the advanced nature of her pregnancy, it asked if she wanted the contact details for government and private hospitals near the hotel in Kuala Lumpur.

'Please send them to my phone'. Yi Siang said.

HPL also asked her if she wished to authorise the immediate release of her medical records to any Kuala Lumpur hospital to which she might be admitted. She and Layann discussed this briefly, reaching the conclusion that it was alright. The HPL site registered her acceptance, going on to say that the ITP was still online with more points for communication. They returned to the smiling face, which cheerily said,

'Welcome back to the ITP, Layann and Yi Siang. The road tax on your car expires in three days, on 27 July. I can renew it for you, but your car will need to pass a roadworthiness test first'.

They stared glumly at the screen. Then Yi Siang looked at her husband accusingly. 'Really?' she said.

The guide, which had been quiet while it conducted a search, informed them, 'I can book you into an ITP approved garage for a roadworthiness test once you reach Kuala Lumpur. Would you like me to do this now?'

[2008]

The Interactive Travel Portal continued

They sorted out arrangements for this, after which the guide offered to let the police know of the length of time they would be away. 'This is entirely optional and for your peace of mind while you leave your house empty. If you wish I can put you onto the Police Service Portal, where you can also take up this option directly'.

They decided to tell the guide the dates and received confirmation that the police had the information.

Finally, the guide asked, 'Do you want to see a short, sponsored film on checking that your car is safe for the journey?'

Layann put his hand over the voice link. 'I don't know if I need that really'. he said. Yi Siang treated him to a silent look that led him to lift his hand and say, 'Yes, I'll have a look'.

The next day they set off on their holiday, content that they were being looked after by so many different agencies which had details of their trip and themselves. Yi Siang picked up the newspaper; the headline read, 'Opinion polls on next month's political elections give a landslide victory to the Fundamentalist National Party [FNP]'. FNP had pledged to clamp down on those falsely claiming benefits or not seeking employment or involved in antisocial activities. It intimated that it would use existing agency information systems to identify such individuals.

[Adapted from Transformed lives?—A future for government electronic service delivery, Electronic Government Services for the 21st Century, Crown Copyright, 2000, pp. 16–17]

Typical Timelines

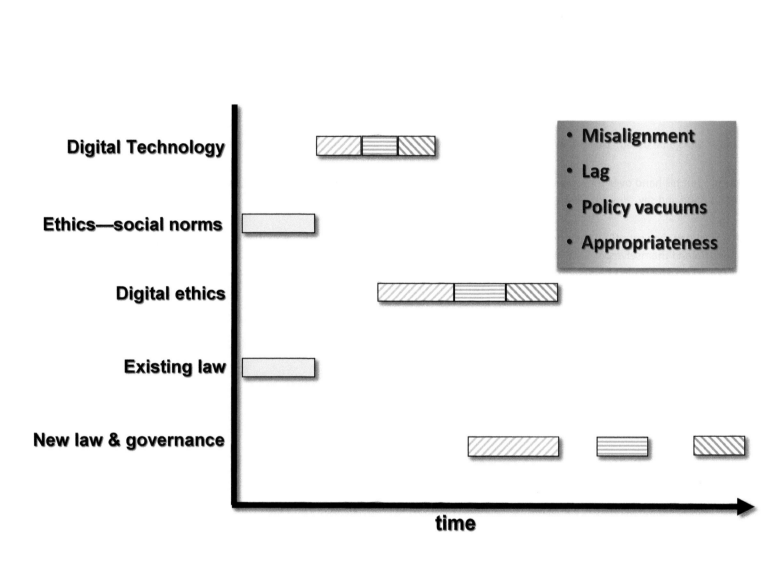

you must always be
Secure
in the Knowledge
that Your
Privacy
Exists!

Skype Ethics [2008]

Points to Ponder

E

Reactive Legislation

The Online Safety Bill is a piece of reactive legislation following many horrendous acts that have occurred in the online world. This legislation is too late for the many who have suffered online—suffering which inevitably spilled over into their day-to-day existence and sadly, for some, ended in death.

Such legislation has started to appear across the world, but it is too late and takes the wrong approach in ensuring that our ever-increasing dependency on digital technology is beneficial and not devastating.

Social impact consideration needs to sit alongside technological development so that early warnings occur and, in turn, trigger timely proactive legislation and governance. Will this happen? Only if there is a widespread shift in thinking, driven by new approaches to education and awareness.

Published in: Voices, The Independent, Wednesday 9 Feb 2022

[2022]

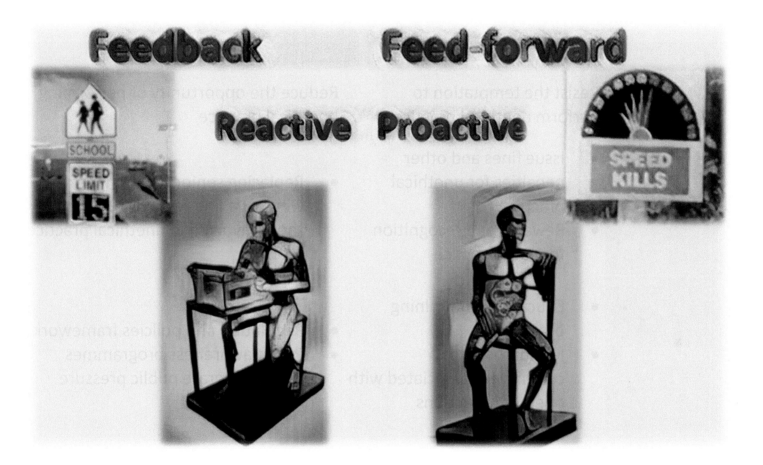

[1999]

R

Taking Ethical Measures

	SIDE ONE	SIDE TWO
	Resist the temptation to perform unethical practice	Reduce the opportunity of performing unethical practice
REACTIVE	• Issue fines and other penalties for unethical practice • Rewards and recognition for good practice	• Replacing senior decision makers who have line responsibility for those involved in unethical practice
PROACTIVE	• Education and training programmes • Mandatory ethics committees associated with operational actions	• Regulation and policies frameworks • Public awareness programmes which generate public pressure

[2017]

 [2019]

Nancy's Ethical Dilemma

Quality Technology Solutions (QTS) was a major well-respected computer hardware and software vendor. Nancy Johnson worked as a user-support software engineer at the QTS regional centre in the middle of the country. She communicated with her customers mainly by telephone and email. Reported program bugs were passed on to technical support agents, and Nancy provided software patches to her customers over telephone lines, usually via a computer-to-computer connection.

In addition, whenever Nancy heard about difficult software problems, she visited the customer personally. Until last year, her on-site support and occasional training were provided as part of the customers' maintenance contracts. As a result of Nancy's expertise, this service became very popular and thus very costly for QTS, so the on-site support service was split from maintenance and billed separately.

During a recent economic recession, QTS's fortunes declined. As a result, salaries were frozen for 18 months. After that, times continued to be difficult, and people were losing their jobs. Nancy believed that it was only a matter of time before she became a casualty. She knew, however, that she was still valuable to QTS, and her boss had said that she would be the first to get a pay raise when it became possible.

One of QTS's largest customers, and one of Nancy's most important clients, was District Benefit (DB), with offices throughout the country. Over a period of time she had established a close relationship with many key employees at DB offices, and there were several offices where employees needed a lot of technical help and training. DB preferred to enter into a contract with QTS, rather than develop its own in-house expertise. Nancy had been working closely with Mike Williams in the Information Services Department of DB, and they know each other well and had high professional respect for each other.

Last week, Mike telephoned Nancy at home.

'Nancy, I have a proposition you might be interested in'.

'What is it?'

'The main office needs someone to help them with their new system. It's the new BENEFIT-p system that QTS installed six months ago and they desperately need support and training. It is the sort of thing you're expert at. Do you want to take it on?'

'It sounds interesting. Just send some details to the office and I'll put the wheels in motion'.

'Let me explain. We don't want QTS to handle the job; we want you to do it personally. If we go to QTS, it will take ages to set it up, and what's more we will have to pay QTS's overhead'.

'I'm not sure, Mike. You're offering to pay me for the type of work which QTS pays me for, and that feels like a conflict of interest'.

[1995]

Nancy's Ethical Dilemma continued

'I don't think so, and we want you to do the job, not some other consultant who might be allocated by QTS. DB is important to QTS, particularly the work at the main office. I'm sure if we explained the situation to your management they would agree to go along with the arrangement'.

'Why don't we then? What's the rush? Put a proposal to them and maybe they can sort something out in a couple of weeks'.

'Nancy, you don't understand. We can't wait that long! BENEFIT-p was installed to rectify serious problems that we were having in managing the complex benefits package. We simply have to have it working in the very near future. We won't ask you for any time that would interfere with your normal work schedule at QTS. We'll fit in with your schedule because we know you'll do a great job. To make it worth your while, we'll pay you 25% above the normal rate and give you a 30% bonus on completion of the job. Please come and work for us on this one job'.

Nancy said nothing. She was pleased that her reputation was so good, and she was overwhelmed by the size of the financial offer. It would certainly provide some extra funds if she were to be let go by QTS. But she wondered about the consequences if QTS were to find out, and she was undecided about what to do.

[1995]

Process and Product

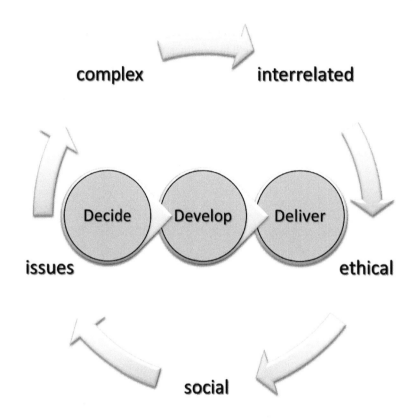

[2010]

Product

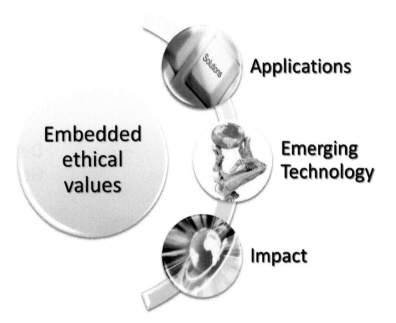

Applications

Embedded ethical values

Emerging Technology

Impact

[2010]

Process

Virtuous action

Education & Training

Design & Governance

Conduct

[2010]

Virtuous Action by Everyone

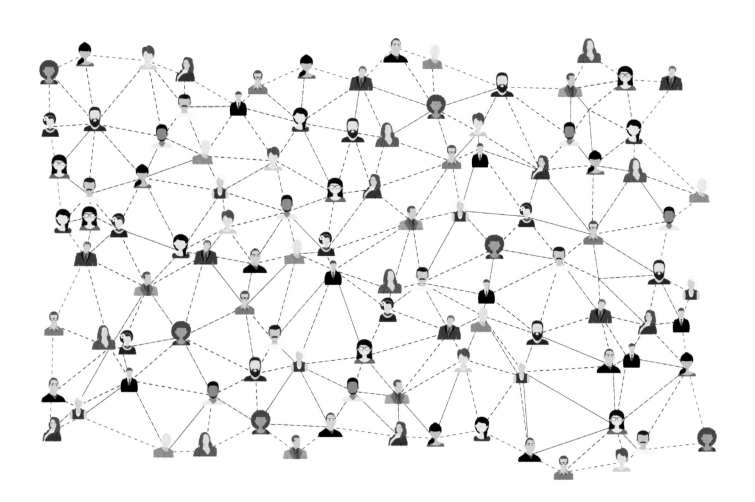

[2022]

Interaction and Communication

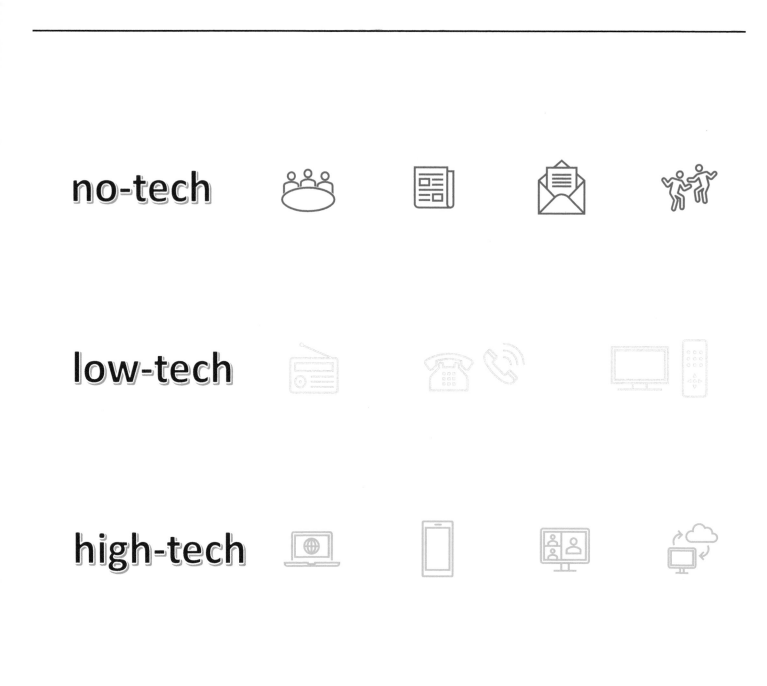

no-tech

low-tech

high-tech

[2021]

Key Ethical Issues in the Information Age

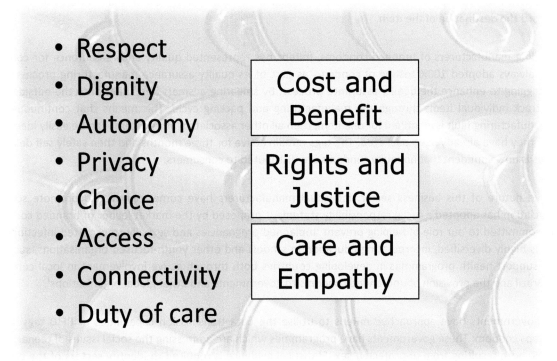

- Respect
- Dignity
- Autonomy
- Privacy
- Choice
- Access
- Connectivity
- Duty of care

| Cost and Benefit |
| Rights and Justice |
| Care and Empathy |

[2008]

Smart Dust of the Brave New World

In the last ten years the manufacturing processes of the chemical and healthcare products industry have become more reliable through increasing reliance on technological tracking, monitoring and testing. In particular, advances in radio frequency identification (RFID) have significantly enhanced tracking and quality assurance in production lines.

RFID is a method of remotely storing and retrieving data using devices called RFID tags, which are minute, ranging from as large as a grain of sand to as small as a speck of dust. RFID tags contain antenna which transmit data held in the tags, such as a unique identity number. This data is processed to, for example, locate the tagged item, check that the item has undergone all the manufacturing processes and record the destination of the item.

As one of the leading manufacturers of branded condoms, mReps has represented quality and reassurance for consumers for many years. mReps has always adopted 100% testing of condoms as part of its quality assurance manufacturing process. Two years ago it introduced RFID tagging to enhance the quality assurance process. By smearing a 'smart dust' RFID onto the outside of each condom, mReps can now track individual items through the manufacturing and packing cycle. This means that continuous checking can be performed. If a manufacturing fault is identified for one item, then all other associated 'at risk' items can be easily identified, located and destroyed, even if they have already been packaged. The tags remain active for three months and then safely self destruct. In using this technology, mReps is now confident that no faulty condoms are distributed to consumers.

Given the sensitive nature of this business sector, individual manufacturers have come together to promote social responsibility. Recently this association has adopted a social responsibility statement proposed by the market leader of branded condoms. This states, 'We are strongly committed to our role of helping prevent unplanned pregnancies and sexually transmitted infections worldwide. Our work in this area is highly diversified, incorporating education in schools and other youth-focused organisations, such as the Outward Bound Trust. We support health programmes in developing countries both through active involvement in local communities, such as Programme H in Brazil and the provision of unbranded condoms to governments and other global organisations'.

Recently several governments have approached mReps to utilise the data transmission capabilities of RFID tags smeared onto the outside of the mReps condom. These governments have programmes which are addressing the social issues of teenage pregnancies and the spread of AIDS, both resulting from unprotected sex. Statistical evidence is required to identify sectors of the population who use condoms so that education and programmes can be more targeted. By using RFID data and linking this with national identity proximity card data, it will be possible to compile the necessary demographic consumer data to launch the targeted programmes.

The senior management of mReps meet today to decide if and how they can support this innovative idea.

[2005]

Smart Dust of the Brave New World continued

Public outcry as US lawyer uses Smart Dust data to secure massive divorce settlement

The court in Boston MA today witnessed massive public civil rights demonstration over the use of data from RFID tags on the condoms manufactured by mReps. In an acrimonious celebrity divorce trial between actress Maggie May and rock star Bobby Shafto, lawyer for Ms May, Lex Sphynks successfully proved Shafto and Ms X had had sexual intercourse. The so-called smart dust tag on a condom purchased by Shafto had been transmitting from within Ms X and this had been accidentally picked up by routine surveillance monitoring at Boston International Airport. Shafto and Ms X claimed their civil rights had been abused but nevertheless Shafto agreed a settlement to Ms May of $8million. . .

Thursday's edition of the Boston Bugle, Page 3

H

[2005]

Information Dichotomy

lifeblood

pollution

[2011]

We have become information junkies who feed on the byte-size trivia. [2000]

Communication without moral application is at best a wasted opportunity and at worst a dangerous threat to society and the rights of its citizens. [2003]

An empowering Information Society must be founded upon ethical ICT [2008]

Points to Ponder

F

Did I really meet President Bill Clinton?

BB

[1998]

Information Provenance

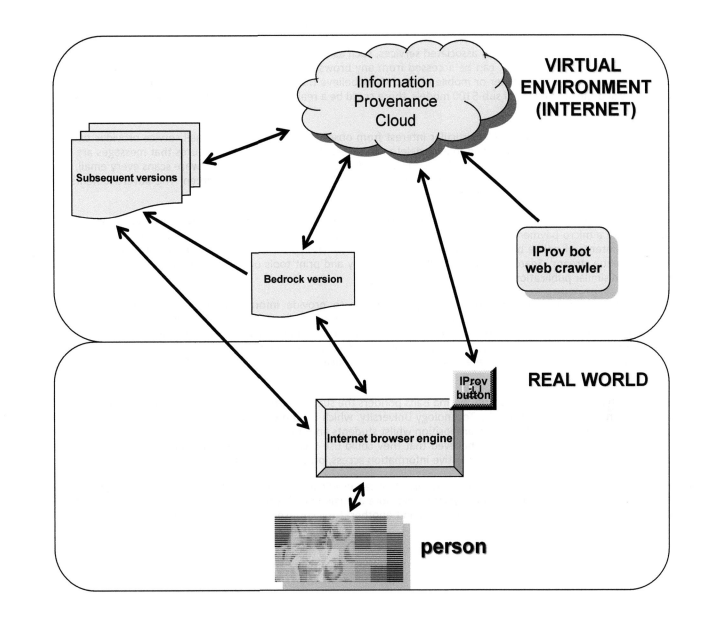

[2010]

The Favourite Search Engine

Search-IT is fast becoming the world's favourite search engine. Last month it cornered 32% of worldwide website traffic of those looking for information or online shopping services. Since its inception, Search-IT has focused almost exclusively on providing services that are platform independent. Its search engine and associated services, such as Search-IT Groups, Search-IT Images, Search-IT News, Search-IT Mail, Search-IT Talk and Search-IT Maps, can be accessed from any browser. Search-IT's objective is to make all possible information available to everyone who has a computer or mobile phone. Many believe that Search-IT offers untold riches because, with the falling cost of computers and the imminence of sub-$100 models, there could be a real opportunity to close the digital divide—within countries and between them.

Some of Search-IT's services have attracted particular interest from observers. Search-IT's web-mail service provides two gigabytes of storage to each subscriber, removing any need to ever delete messages. The Search-IT server ensures that messages are securely kept forever. This web-mail service is free because it is funded by advertising. In return Search-IT's software scans every email, identifies key phrases, and puts what it regards as relevant advertisements on the right-hand side of the screen. The advertisements selected for display are logged so that advertisers can be billed.

The Search-IT search engine is predicated on the fact that most of its sources are accessed for nothing. This is because content providers are unable to devise a micro-payment system to activate when their data is trawled by a search engine. This search process has been extended to the contents of online books. Search-IT argues that authors should view their inclusion as a free marketing tool that can 'deliver a new revenue stream'. Search-IT automatically disables copy and print tools on host computers while users are accessing full copies of books and similar publications.

Recently Search-IT has been approached by several governments to provide information or restrict access. A group of senior management at Search-IT has made value judgements concerning these requests. Notably Search-IT has refused to provide one government with data revealing what its users are searching for online. This request was claimed to be part of that government's effort to protect children from online pornography. In contrast, as it expands its using population, Search-IT has complied with some national governments' requests to censor material deemed objectionable by local authorities, reasoning that users getting limited access to content was better than no access.

At her palatial ranch in the heart of Trustvaria, Norma Baits ponders the success of the latest Search-IT functions. Norma and her friend Mark Tyme are both postgraduates from the Technology University, which is renowned for its virtual computer network research. The two friends dreamt up the Search-IT business proposition whilst students and subsequently have ruthlessly turned it into a reality. Both share strong political ideals and have always believed that they could use technology as a political instrument, through, for example, mass targeting for manifesto distribution and selective information access, presentation and editorial.

Norma now believed they were nearly at the point where they can use Search-IT to launch their political campaign to create an elite global government that would side-line national politics, promote a single global secular culture and demand everyone would actively participate in wealth creation. 'Just another 12 months and another 2 million users and we can begin to realise our ideals', thought Norma.

[2005]

Information Age Individuals

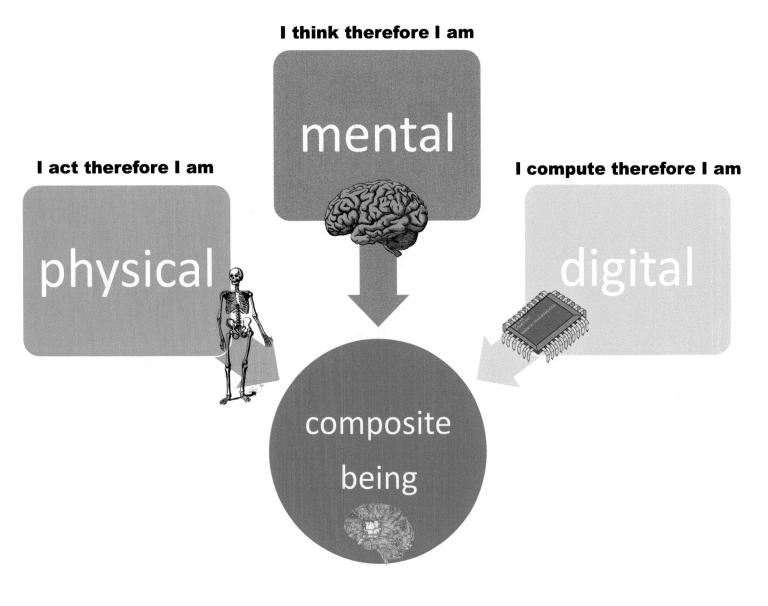

I think therefore I am

mental

I act therefore I am

physical

I compute therefore I am

digital

composite being

[2021]

Is history repeating itself for digital beings?

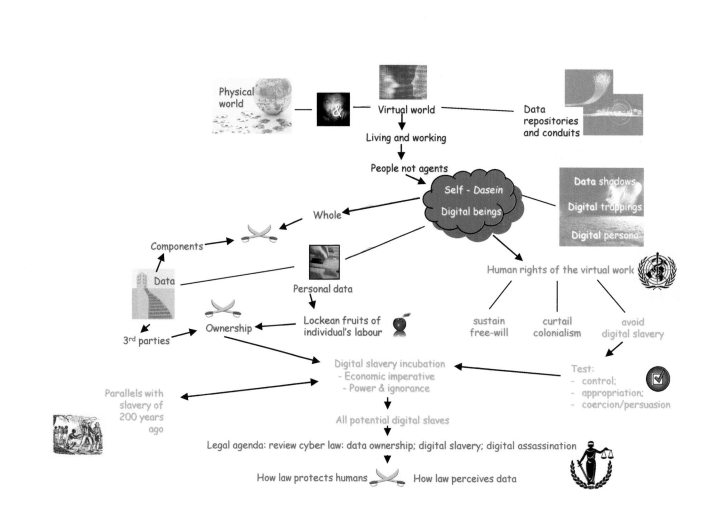

Digital being, the modern way to be,

I am the data and the data is me.

[2016]

The Data Shadow

The afternoon sun beat down from a cloudless sky. Her progress was momentarily recorded as her shadow loitered along behind her. It halted as she stopped to listen to the melodic birdsong. She poured cold water from her water bottle over her hair, and it tickled down her neck as she tried to clear her mind.

What had gone on the night before? She could not remember—it was all an alcoholic haze. She had been woken up late morning by the incessant ring tone of her mobile. It drilled into her brain like an unstoppable pneumatic drill. So many people wanting to be her friend on the social network. And all those messages from her current friends asking if it was true and if it really was her in the video. The video had gone virial—what video?—about what? She simply had no recollection at all. Her identity, once anonymous as Cassandra, had been breached—everyone knew who she really was.

Slowly she walked on. Rounding a corner, a group of teenage boys and girls looked up, pointed at her and giggled. Now she and her shadow moved on quickly, trying to ignore the comments the group cried out after her. It simply would not go away—day after day after day; posted message after posted message after posted message. So much data, so many untruths accepted as fact. And then it was gone—the social network crashed. It was no longer the place to be, no longer cool, no longer where the action was. She hardly dared believe that she had her life back.

The years passed, and memories of that night faded. Examination success, college graduation and a promising career beckoned. She waited patiently for her turn. Well prepared, calmly confident—this was the job she wanted—this was the job she would secure. As she looked around the room, she saw that the other candidates looked nervous, tense—it was hers for the taking if she kept to her game plan. Her name was called. She glided into the room, eyed the panel and smiled at them. Questions asked. Answers given assuredly. It was going well and then it happened.

Could she explain how the video of her some years earlier related and indeed supported the values she had just articulated? That video! How had it been found? She was not aware that about a year ago the founders of the social network had bought back the rights and had resurrected the 'chat site with attitude' and even managed to reinstate many of the old threads, pictures and videos. They were there for anyone to access. Once again, she was infamous, but this time her infamy was all pervasive, as messages had spread across the many social networks that now existed in the online world. Self-confidence drained. The panel now seemed like both judge and jury. Dreams of a meteoric career shattered.

The afternoon sun beat down from a cloudless sky. Her progress was momentarily recorded as her shadow loitered along behind her, and then it was gone forever. But not so her data shadow. It would remain permanently out there in the digital world of bits and bytes. There for all to view. There for all to judge her by.

Looking up at the sun there was a faint smile on her face and tears in her eyes. She now knew what she had to do.

[2017]

Currency

I was what I was

But now I am what I am

Data shadows lie

[2019]

In order to live and prosper in the information age, the cybercitizen must be visible, credible and creditable [2000]

Unlike our shadows in the physical world, our data shadows remain long after we have passed by and are there for all to inspect and report on [2003]

In the not-too-distant future with the cloud, big data, and maybe 80–90 per cent of the world's population online and connected, the scope for systems of oppression seems limitless [2015]

Points to Ponder

G

Digital flume

---

pandemic gloom

dark days loom

funerial smoke plume

humankind doom

then despair entomb

enter new broom

ideas bloom

communication womb

birth to room and Zoom

digital boom

we all consume

H

Sky Travel

For three years Sky Travel, the leading high street travel agency in the country, saw profits fall alarmingly. Some argue that this was due to a worldwide decline in overseas holiday sales, whilst others argue that it was due to increasing competition from other firms that have seen the potential of the Internet to increase market share in sales of cheap flights and package holidays.

Sky Travel decided to follow this move and six months ago launched 'Surf and Sun', an Internet-based service aimed at the cheaper and younger end of the market. Surf and Sun was an instant success. In the six months of trading since its launch, sales have increased by 12% and profits increased by 13.5%. Sky Travel believes it has turned the business around and avoided a potentially catastrophic downward spiral in its profits.

In setting up Surf and Sun, Sky Travel sought advice from a range of people, including those already involved in electronic trading, those providing Internet information services, those using the Internet as resource to support employees and those providing the tools for and access to the Internet. On the basis of this research, Sky Travel established some key principles on which to build Surf and Sun.

- Development of the new service would be done in-house—new expertise would be hired as none existed within the current workforce.

- The new service would be integrated with the existing high street service. Staff would be retrained and expected to do both types of job as requested.

- An emphasis would be placed on increasing the online service at the expense of the face-to-face service on the grounds of cost.

- Staff would be rewarded under a new bonus scheme based on optimum performance across both types of service.

- Staff would be penalised by loss of bonuses for abuse of Internet access through, for example, personal surfing and private email. Persistent abuse would be the subject of formal disciplinary action.

- Electronic financial transactions related to sales via Surf and Sun would be handled by a third party directly linked into the in-house network.

One of the key points stressed by existing electronic traders and service providers was the need to optimise bandwidth usage. Sky Travel was told that it needed to safeguard against potential misuse of Internet access for email activity and for downloading inappropriate files such as MP3s. There was a legal compliance issue, but more important, 'private usage' could bring a service to a standstill because of bandwidth limitations. Sky Travel was strongly advised to implement functions which would reduce the risk of such occurrences. The additional advantage of doing this was that employees would also be protected from receiving compromising spam emails and other files. Several organisations explained they had successfully 'sold' this idea to the workforce using this argument rather than the employee misuse argument.

[2005]

Sky Travel continued

This ~~had~~ greatly influenced the way Sky Travel had developed its new online service. A firewall and web filter software were installed. The filter enabled all traffic to be monitored and non-essential files types such as MP3, streaming media and Internet gaming to be blocked. A database of unacceptable material was maintained and updated by the software vendor in consultation with Sky Travel. In association with this filter, all employees were issued with an Acceptable Use Policy statement.

Whilst unhappy with the way new work practices had been introduced, employees of Sky Travel reluctantly accepted the new operation. Six months on and the company was showing an upturn, but there was a cost. Staff were becoming increasingly stressed by the monitoring, although a management representative had stated to the press that, 'We don't want to watch our employees' every move but merely want to ensure that we are using our network appropriately. All our employees understand this and are benefiting overall by the upturn in our business'.

Five days ago Surf and Sky started to suffer a degradation of service. Management asked the technical experts to check the monitoring data from the filter. They looked carefully through all the data and opened up many emails of employees on the basis of some tentative predictions made by the filter. The technical staff could find nothing. Management issued a strong statement to all staff reminding them of the consequences of abuse of Internet facilities and that this could jeopardise the future of the company. Three days ago 10 of the 25 key employees resigned on receiving this statement.

Yesterday morning Surf and Sun was hit by a denial of service attack which closed the service, and as yet it has not returned. But the cause had been found. A hacker had gained access to the network via the third party responsible for handling financial transactions and who had direct connection to the network. No filtering existed of the transactions of the third party as they were seen beyond reproach and totally secure. The hacker had at first caused some degradation of service by using large amounts of bandwidth for short enough periods to remain undetected. The hacker's activity had then escalated to a full and successful denial of service attack. Surf and Sun was closed and could not be re-established until the link for financial transactions was made secure.

[2005]

Digital Technologies and War

[2022]

Digital Technologies and War

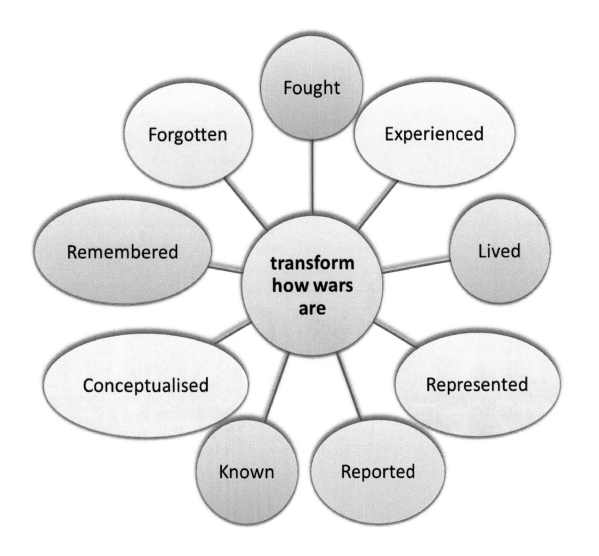

[2022]

Smart City

[2022]

SMART City Ethical Hotspots

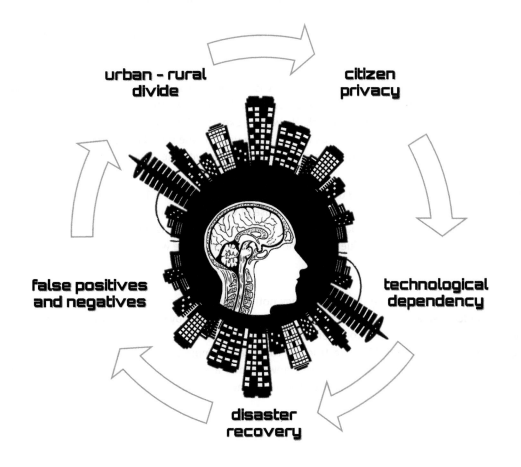

urban - rural divide

citizen privacy

technological dependency

disaster recovery

false positives and negatives

The Bank of Lilliput

The Bank of Lilliput was thought to be a small, perfectly formed bank beyond reproach. That was before the global financial meltdown. It was now in difficulty, caught up in the financial turmoil which was not of its doing. Rumours were rife of impending redundancies as Lilliput struggled to remain intact. It had long been totally reliant upon a sophisticated ICT infrastructure, which was supported by 500 ICT professionals across a range of specialisms and geographic locations. These 500 professionals were viewed by the industry as being the best there was. Lilliput had paid high salaries and bonuses to keep these staff and had provided first-class staff development opportunities.

The rumour was that ICT was an area were Lilliput could make vast financial savings in these troubled times. Brad Quatermass was a senior systems engineer who was becoming increasingly worried about his position. The rumours that job cuts were looming sent Brad looking for a redundancy list within the company network. He was an expert in his field and so knew how to use the ICT infrastructure without being traced. He accessed personnel systems as well as those used by the Board of the bank in his search. Eventually he found it—a detailed list of those who could be potentially made redundant together with the cost of doing so and the savings to be made.

Associated with this list was also a strategy of how the company could still operate its ICT effectively with only 50% of the ICT staff. Brad was dismayed not only because his name was on the list but because of when the list and strategy had been drawn up. He had examined the properties of the documents and associated databases, and it was clear that this action had been first considered 18 months ago, at a time when Lilliput was publicly heralding the value of its in-house ICT expertise. He wondered how the Board could treat its staff in this way.

Brad wondered what he should do. It seemed that redundancy notices were to be served on 50% of ICT staff within four weeks. There would then be a lot of people looking for new jobs in a job market which was already in decline. Brad reasoned that it was a time to look after himself. What would make him attractive to potential employers ahead of other candidates? And then he realised—information. He embarked on a systematic trawl of the ICT infrastructure to extract competitive corporate data, including customer and contact databases as well as financial product information. He also downloaded access/password codes and encryption/decryption keys. He planned to use this information as a negotiating tool to secure his next post on being made redundant. Now information rich, he covered all his electronic tracks and waited.

[2008]

The Bank of Lilliput continued

Two weeks later the Bank of Lilliput announced that, due to the global financial crisis, it reluctantly had been forced in the last month to downscale its operation dramatically. As a result it was going to make 50% of its ICT staff redundant—a move it regretted and until very recently had never envisaged would ever happen.

Staff were devastated. Brad listened without emotion. Inwardly he felt vindicated—how could Lilliput treat staff in this was and publicly lie about its actions? Tomorrow he would make his phone calls to the competitors in the financial sector he had identified as needing his expertise as well as the information that he had stashed in an online encrypted storage website. He would take the redundancy money and then start his new job. What happened to his colleagues, he did not know and did not care. He thought some of them may have already collected information as well.

Immediately after the announcement, ICT staff found all the access protocols had been changed, and those made redundant were escorted off the premises.

L

[2008]

Drone Dichotomy

[2022]

Future Genus

Bowed heads

Worship smart deities

Thumbs at the ready

Unaware of surroundings

Virtually addicted

Goodbye world

All hail the god cyber

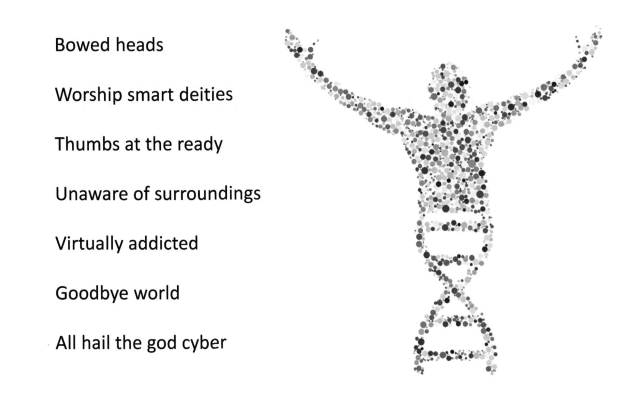

[2022]

Digital Divide

For digital natives the move to the virtual is plausible and possibly pleasurable,
but for digital outcasts the move is fraught and frequently frightening.

[2020]

The day when the technology is transparent will be the day people have been put first [2001]

Inequitable access to and communication of the priceless resource of information is at best unfair and at worst disastrous for society as a whole [2004]

We all deserve fit-for-purpose systems by design and not by luck, that will sustain and empower us [2011]

H

The Hacker

Black hat cracker on the offensive

White hat hacker on the defensive

Sitting on the fence grey hat mercenary pensive

All brothers and sisters with one common objective

Discover network and computer security how effective

But reasons differ between black and white hats

Vulnerabilities exploited or identified

Organisations attacked or protected

Security breached or enhanced

The hacker—which side of the digital technology coin?

[2022]

4 Forward Looking

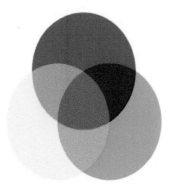

It is impossible to reverse the technology; the important thing is to ask questions before you have a problem. [2000]

Points to Ponder

remember the people

one solution is no solution

[2009]

It is time to start a revolution in your head which will culminate in ethical computing by everyone for everyone. [2020]

The simple digital ethics message for corporates is *Put People Before Profit* and in politics is *Put People Before Party.* [2021]

In the digital age it is people who change things. It is people who make digital technology. It is people who use and abuse digital technology. [2021]

Points to Ponder

J

Project management should be guided by a sense of justice, a sense of equal distributions of benefits and burdens and a sense of equal opportunity. [1996]

Professional codes should not be an instrument of compliance but an instrument of appliance in furthering ethical ICT. [2015]

There is a need to develop a new vision for digital ethics which is theoretically grounded but pragmatic. It must exhibit phronesis and praxis, so that industry and government will engage, accept and embrace this as a modus operandi. [2021]

K

Lifelong-learning Partnership

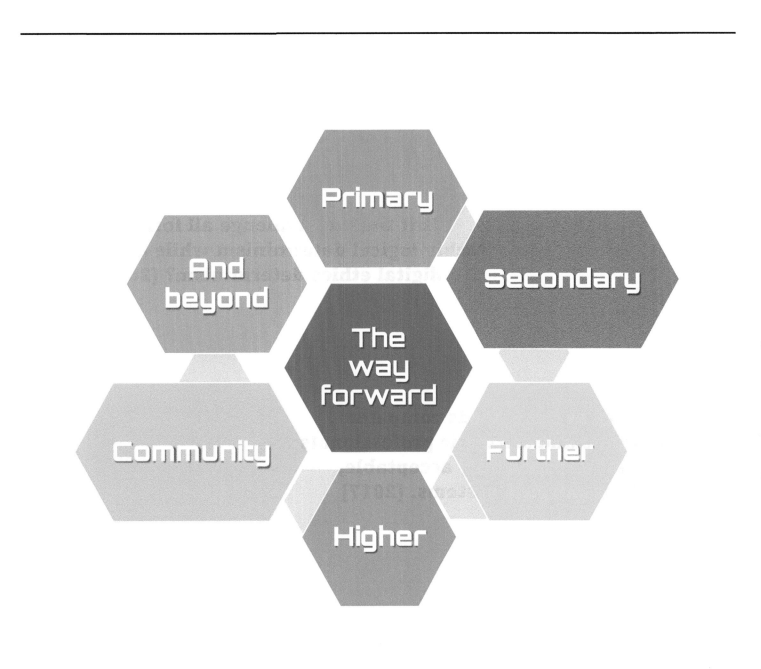

[2022]

Is it time to challenge all forms of technological determinism while accepting digital ethics determinism? [2022]

Society at large needs competent, empathetic and altruistic professionals to deliver societally acceptable, fit-for-purpose systems. [2017]

Points to Ponder

L

Acrostic Analysis

Corporate
Organisations
Must
Promote
Unreservedly
Technological
Ethical
Responsibility

Data
Into
Global
Information
Transforms
All
Lives

Everything
That
Holds
Information
Controls
Society

L

[2021]

Engage and Influence

politically

commercially

industrially

professionally

societally

internationally

[2022]

Digital

Digital age, digital technology, digital people
Digital adds to life
Digital subtracts from life

But why?
Because:

People make things
People change things
People use things
People abuse things

So:

Digital education for everyone

Then:

Digital technology for everyone
Young and old, rich and poor, here and there
Reboot society
Reboot life
Reboot digital!

M

[2021]

Reimagination

progress, mature and influence through a presence in these 11 spheres

[2022]

Present Day

Present Day (PD) is a very successful retail chain which sells a wide range of gifts for that special occasion. It has outlets in major cities around the world and at many of the world's busiest airports. To complement the retail outlets, PD operates Web Shop for those who want gifts delivered to their home or to the person who is to receive the gift. PD's success is built upon a highly motivated workforce determined to provide a quality service to all Present Day customers. It is a contractual requirement that all employees of PD can speak English. This has enabled global communication.

The CEO of PD has growing concerns that there is an increasing divide between staff located in different countries and regions as well as between those associated with the retail outlets and those associated with Web Shop. The reason for her concern is that PD has a common approach across the world, which has established its brand as representing consistent high quality regardless of geographical location. Having local differences will damage PD's brand and reputation, which will lead to loss of competitive advantage.

The decision is taken to implement a PD community-building initiative aimed at bringing people together socially, thus helping to overcome divides. This is based on establishing a social networking site, All Present, which is accessible only to PD employees. It has been agreed that staff can spend up to 15% of their work time using All Present. Staff will have access to All Present from every computer within PD as well as from home or other approved locations.

To get things started, all staff are signed up to All Present. Their basic personal details are transferred across from PD's human resource systems. Staff numbers and dates of birth are used as the User ID and Password. Communications in All Present are kept indefinitely, and everyone can see every communication. The use of All Present was immediate, with over 90% of staff using it within the first week of its launch some six months ago.

However, monitoring of All Present activity has revealed that whilst a community has been established, it is not quite what the CEO had expected. There has been a lot of communications criticising policy and decision-making in PD and suggesting actions that should be taken. People who hold opinions not in line with the 'All Present norm' are hounded and alienated. It also appears that non-PD people are contributing to All Present using existing user ids and passwords. The latest problem is that there has been a successful hack into All Present through a security flaw on the Web Shop site.

The CEO is very surprised and disappointed that All Present has exacerbated divides as well as promoted dissent. She takes the decision to close AP immediately. PD staff are outraged, claiming it is a breach of their human rights. Industrial action is threatened if AP is not reinstated. Meanwhile the AP community migrates to a public social network.

[2007]

M

We must accept and adjust to the fact that we are all technologists to a lesser or greater degree. How we educate our future generations must reflect this change to ensure ethical digital technology is realised. [2022]

When we work with wisdom we will work world wonders! [2022]

Points to Ponder

M

Ethical Digital Technology

Ethical ignorance

Ethical naïvety

Ethical apathy

Ethical blind spots

Ethical hotspots

Ethical awakening

Ethical awareness

Ethical journey

Ethical inclusion

Ethical destination

Ethical Digital Technology

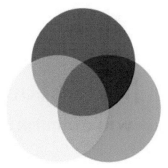

[2022]

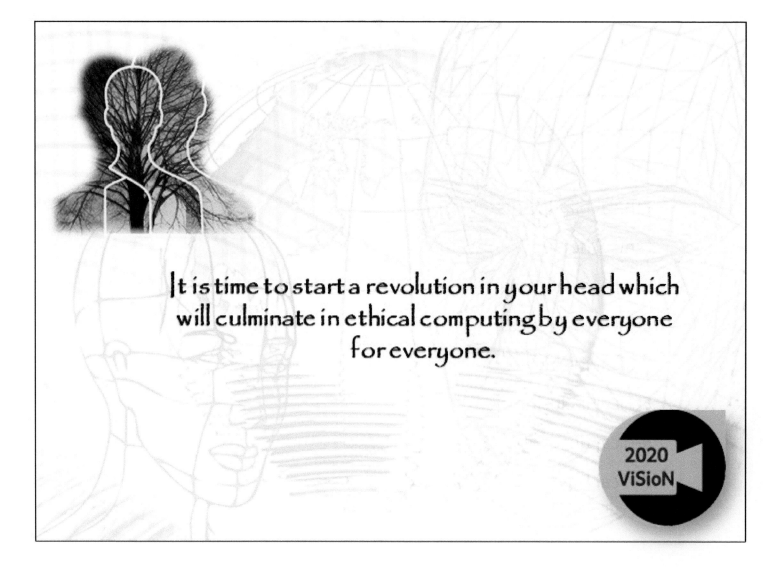

It is time to start a revolution in your head which will culminate in ethical computing by everyone for everyone.

2020 ViSioN

[2020]

5 Food for Thought

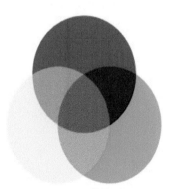

The aim of this book is to encourage readers to draw their own conclusions about the ethical efficacy of digital technology. For this reason, explanations of ideas and issues, which I am trying to convey, have been grouped together in this final section. As mentioned in the introduction, there are four creative forms used in the book: pictures, poems, stories and quotations. In the tables which follow, there are notes for every creative element. The letters in the bottom left hand corner of each element refer to the row in the relevant creative form table. These notes might expand on the theme or pose questions to encourage the reader to think beyond the obvious or provide some insight into how the element was derived.

Two wordles precede the four creative element tables. A wordle is simply a visual representation of words, where the size of each word is proportional to the number of times it appears. The first wordle, which was created by Mary Pahlke, illustrates the foundation on which ethical digital technology should be built. The second wordle depicts the most important topics and concepts discussed in *Ethical Digital Technology in Practice*, the second book in the trilogy. This wordle serves as an interface between the differing perspectives of the books in the trilogy.

Unusually for a book grounded in the academe, words are subservient to images. There is a good reason for this. This book is aimed at everyone. Humans process images in 13 milliseconds, and so visual content engages and helps them understand complicated concepts (Brown, 2018). Therefore, images appear not only in the picture creative form but also in the other three creative forms. Most of the poems have associated images. When a poem and an image work in tandem, the resulting combination takes on an entirely new, deeper meaning (Photory, 2022).

References

Brown, S. (2018). *What is the Impact of Visual Content Marketing?* Rocktetium, July 19. Retrieved November 20, 2022, from https://rocketium.com/academy/impact-visual-content-marketing/

Photory (2022). *Photopoetry: An Artistic Blend of Poetry and Image.* Visual Storytelling Community blog. Retrieved November 20, 2022, from https://www.photory.app/blogs/blend-poetry-with-image/

Image by Mary Pahlke from Pixabay

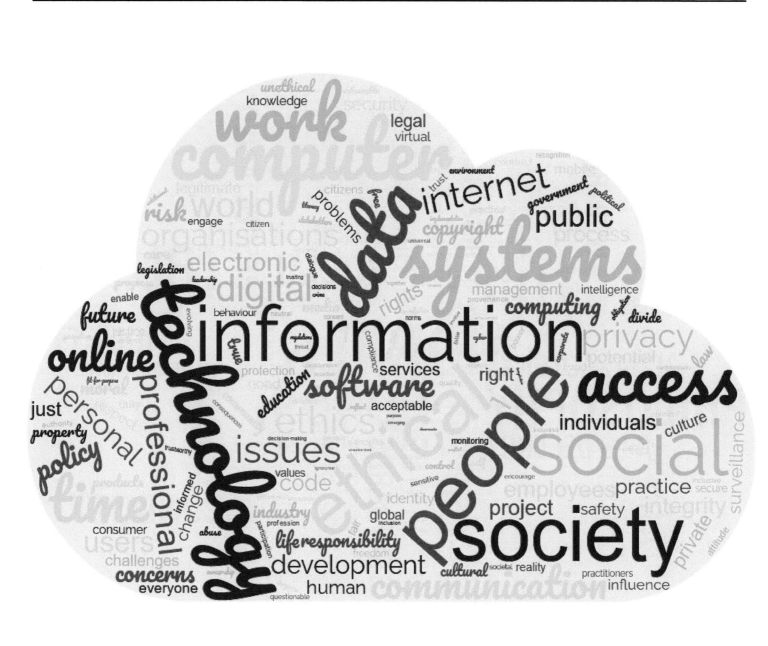

Picture

A	The transition of STEM (Science, Technology, Engineering, and Mathematics) to STEAM (Science, Technology, Engineering, Arts and Mathematics) aims to promote creativity and curiosity. However, we must not forget social responsibility.
B	The language of digital technology is dominated by acronyms. This creates barriers for those not involved in developing and delivering the technology.
C	The practical application of ethics across the development and application of digital technology is paramount. This should take into account the broader societal settings often explored and defined through the social sciences.
D	In the digital age, the social sciences possibly need to be realigned to ensure they remain effective, interrelated analysis tools.
E	Follow the timeline. What will it happen in the next five years?
F	Emergent digital technology has resulted in easier access by a greater range of people.
G	Have converging technologies resulted in empowering communication across society for everyone or a selected few?
H	Many actions can be defined logically. If so, they are then capable of being computerised. The first step is to define the logical flow of the action explicitly.
I	Digital technology applications comprise not only the technology but also the people who use those applications.
J	An early example of a digital technology application system comprising professionals from different specialisms, measuring equipment as well as the digital technology hardware and software.
K	The 1970s energy crisis led to substantial fuel shortages as well as elevated prices. Companies turned to computerised vehicle scheduling systems to optimise transport cost through a significant reductions in mileage.
L	Digital technology has a history of trends and media hype. Artificial intelligence appears to be the latest.
M	The management of digital technology projects is complex and demanding. This schematic was originally published in Rogerson, S. (1989). *Project Skills Handbook*. Chartwell-Bratt, p.20.
N	Trust is challenging to achieve and easy to be lost as digital technology is implemented.

Picture

O	A rich picture shows the existing tensions in creating a code of conduct for a professional body with digital technology. In soft systems methodology, a rich picture is a cartoon-like picture used to capture the complexities and nuances of a real-world situation.
P	A rich picture shows the typical complex interactions within the system development process. There are many ethical dilemmas across this landscape.
Q	Accepting our societal obligations and responsibilities is important because misalignment of these timelines will always exist.
R	To reduce the likelihood of problematic digital technology, there needs to be feed-forward processes incorporated in design and installation.
S	Societal responsibilities and obligations are best supported through temptations being both reduced and resisted.
T	Personal data should not be collected in a fanciful manner.
U	Addressing both the processes and products of digital technology is necessary for realising a successful conclusion.
V	Product concerns the outcome of professional endeavour and whether digital technology systems are deemed to be ethically viable. This is a teleological perspective.
W	Process concerns the activities of practitioners and whether their conduct is deemed virtuous. This is a deontological perspective.
X	We all have responsibilities towards society.
Y	Not everyone uses high tech. So why is high tech seen by many as the perfect future?
Z	Decisions taken regarding digital technology on the basis of only cost–benefit analysis is a flawed approach. There is much more that needs to be taken into account.
AA	Information is double sided.
BB	As a younger man did I meet Bill Clinton the then President of the United States? Here is the evidence. However—this picture is a fake! The ability to manipulate pictures digitally can be amusing, but it can be very dangerous, damaging, hurtful and deceitful.

Picture

CC	Information provenance would fix the origin and network of ownership, thus providing a measure of integrity, authenticity and trustworthiness. Information provenance offers a normative instrument for turning the moral obligation of addressing information integrity into ethical practice.
DD	Are you a composite being living in the multi-facetted digital age?
EE	When personal data is harvested without restriction, it becomes an instrument of digital slavery in the hands of the unscrupulous. This rich picture explores this issue.
FF	Wars rage across the world. The devastation in Ukraine is the latest tragedy in the history of humanity.
GG	With the advent of digital technology, modern warfare has become even more complex and far reaching. The human cost is colossal.
HH	Smart cities have their own set of hotspots. What might they be and what about rural areas?
II	Are drones a good thing or a bad thing?
JJ	The digital divide continues to exist. What can be done to remove this so everyone can benefit from advances in digital technology?
KK	Often digital technology is put before people when strategic decisions are made. The fact is often ignored that we all have different needs, different skills and different preferences.
LL	Throughout our lives, we must all continue to learn and be aware of the consequences of digital technology.
MM	The digital technology landscape is vast. Which part do you travel in?
NN	How could you make a difference and contribute to realising ethical digital technology?

Poem

A	A list poem—The ethical digital technology landscape described in a three-sided alphabet.
B	A list poem—Some details of information and communication technology (ICT). ICT is termed *digital technology* in this trilogy.
C	A rhyming couplet poem—The poem forms the comments for the computer programme pseudocode. It describes the logic in a creative way.
D	Three haiku poems linked together—A call to address technological dependency in an inclusive manner.
E	Three haiku poems linked together—Has evolution reached the final chapter?
F	One rhyming couplet—You are your personal data.
G	A haiku poem—Data shadows last forever. Is this a problem?
H	A rhyme poem—The pandemic caused digital dependency to increase worldwide. Is this a positive or a negative to come out of the pandemic?
I	An acrostic poem—A warning about the hype surrounding advancing technology.
J	A free verse poem—Are we addicted to ~~the~~ technology? Could you live without digital technology?
K	A rhyme poem—Cybersecurity is one of the biggest issues in the digital age. The role of the hacker is double sided.
L	An acrostic poem—Some pointers on how to move forward in terms of organisations and the issues surrounding data and information.
M	A free verse poem—The digital age is challenging!
N	A list poem—The journey from ethical ignorance to ethical achievement. When, if ever, will this be fulfilled?

Story

A	*Chimerical* means filled with idle fancies and wild dreams; whimsical, fanciful. An algorithm is a logical set of instructions used to solve problems or perform tasks.
B	An account of the technological landscape which seems to hold true today. The challenges and warning signs were apparent in 1988. Extract from Rogerson, S. (1988). *The World of Information Technology, Graduate Scientist and Engineer,* Vol. 9, No. 6. pp. 50–51.
C	Computerised production control is well established. The wider implications should not be overlooked during the system development process.
D	Is the business model for GARAGE ethical? Who has the moral responsibility for the woman's death? What role does technology play in this situation? What would you now do if you were Wendy?
E	Powerful persuasive technology can sustain top-down control and facilitate subliminal coercion.
F	Whilst emergency calls for reactive action, proactive forethought can prevent the occurrence of emergency.
G	What would you do in Nancy's position? Does it make any difference that there is uncertainty about Nancy's current job? Who does Nancy have a responsibility towards? Does she have a responsibility towards herself and her family?
H	Were the decisions of the mReps Board of Managers ethically responsible? If, yes, why do you think so? If no, why do you think not? What should be done when new digital technology products are invented?
I	Search engines have become an accepted tool across the whole of society. Those controlling these tools are globally powerful. It is an example of how technology has become a significant political instrument which has associated dangers.
J	Should we be more wary of the risks associated with data shadows? What could organisations do to reduce the risk of inappropriate personal data existing online, particularly if this existence is permanent? What could individuals do to safeguard the integrity of their online personal data? What responsibilities and obligations do computing professionals have regarding the creation and existence of data shadows?
K	An early example of the challenges of cybersecurity. The complexity of ethically charged issues includes outsourcing and workforce vetting and monitoring.
L	Banks have become totally dependent on digital technology. Professionals working in this area are in positions of power, influence and responsibility. There are demands on both employers and employees to ensure ethical integrity.
M	This global human activity system incorporates many different cultures and social groupings. Is social media an effective vehicle for supporting cultural diversity? How could the CEO's action plan be modified to realise cultural harmony?

Quotation

A		Don't be constrained by convention and tradition whilst at the same time being aware of them.
B		Have you experienced both the positives and negatives of digital technology?
C		Digital technology projects are surrounded by many challenging issues which are often overlooked.
D		The attractiveness of digital technology has resulted in a dependency which has coloured society in both positive and negative ways.
E		The terms and conditions of use for all social media platforms often hide serious ethical issues.
F		Is the information society a reality or a myth?
G		Our data profiles will permanently colour our lives whether we like it or not.
H		It's so easy to forget the people.
I		More often than not, the permanency of digital technology goes unnoticed. Disaster beckons!
J		A new approach is called for which is adopted by all.
K		The scope of consideration needs to go beyond the technical area. Compliance can be superficial.
L		Is this a pipe dream or a new order?
M		We, as technologists, must think before we act.
N		Stop and rethink.

9781032422176